OUR JESUIT LIFE

Our
Jesuit
Life

ST. LOUIS
THE INSTITUTE OF JESUIT SOURCES
1990

The material in this volume from the Formula of the Institute, the General Examen, and the Constitutions is taken from *The Constitutions of the Society of Jesus,* translated with an Introduction and Commentary by George E. Ganss, S.J. (Saint Louis: The Institute of Jesuit Sources, 1970).

The Orientations from the General Congregations and the Fathers General and the Practical Rules come from the following sources: *Documents of the Thirty-First and Thirty-Second General Congregations of the Society of Jesus,* edited by John W. Padberg, S.J. (Saint Louis: The Institute of Jesuit Sources, 1977); *Documents of the Thirty-Third General Congregation of the Society of Jesus,* edited by Donald R. Campion, S.J., and Albert C. Louapre, S.J. (Saint Louis: The Institute of Jesuit Sources, 1984); and *Acta Romana Societatis Jesu* (Roma: Apud Curiam Praepositi Generalis). The volumes of *Acta Romana* are noted at the respective quotations.

First Edition

© 1990 The Institute of Jesuit Sources
   3700 West Pine Blvd.
   Saint Louis, MO 63108
   314-652-5737

ISBN 912422-98-X

CONTENTS

PART TWO
ORIENTATIONS FROM THE GENERAL CONGREGATIONS AND THE FATHERS GENERAL

PART THREE
PRACTICAL RULES

FOREWORD BY FATHER GENERAL

With the approach of the Ignatian year, I am happy to offer you *Our Jesuit Life*. In addition to the Formula of the Institute, the book consists of three major parts, "Readings from the General Examen and from the Constitutions of the Society of Jesus," "Orientations from the General Congregations and the Fathers General," and "Practical Rules." You will see that this is a new edition of the two earlier collections which Fr. Pedro Arrupe put out some years ago, "Readings from the Constitutions" and "Jesuit Religious Life." They remain fundamentally unchanged here, especially the first of them, "Readings from the Constitutions."

The second of the earlier collections, which was entitled "Jesuit Religious Life," does however show certain important modifications in the present volume, the better to stress mission as central to our life. The first two chapters of "Orientations" are dedicated to mission and a final one is added on our maintenance and growth as a missionary body. So that the book may be fully authoritative, the only texts used are from the decrees of General Congregations or from the letters of the Superiors General to the whole Society.

The third part of this book, "Practical Rules," takes the place of the former "Common Rules," in the same way that the "Readings from the Constitutions" replace the former "Summary" of the Constitutions.

Our Jesuit Life is set out as a rule, but a rule that is in the service of life. The orientations and norms seek to ensure for the Society its proper unity, effectiveness and identity. St. Ignatius, in various parts of the Spiritual Exercises and the Constitutions, affirms that every spiritual impulse requires assistance from the written word; if we would fulfill the spirit, the letter must not be abolished. In like manner, according to him, the preservation of the apostolic body of the Society needs a rule, concretely.

However, a spirituality like that of Ignatius, constantly searching for *greater* knowledge and service of the Lord, can never be held up by the letter of a law or be content with mere observance of what is prescribed. For this reason, St. Ignatius has entrusted to the Society the smallest number of rules but the highest demands to love and serve the Lord in all things.

The contemplation of the Word made man was for St. Ignatius the way to learn the divine art of living within the vast horizons of Him who is the Way, the Truth, and the Life and of incarnating the desires inspired in us by this contemplation within the restrictions of our everyday, here and now, concrete living and working, as a practical effort at solidarity with the apostolic body of the Society.

This is why *Our Jesuit Life* is not a rule-book, although like the Constitutions it certainly contains normative elements. Its aim is to open the Society to a dynamic vision of the work to be done in the Lord's company for the "aid of souls," watchful that the vision does not remain a mere dream nor the Society reduce itself to a theory for want of providing the Spirit with a body, a written word and a rule. The selection of texts that we present today contains that tension which Ignatius's Constitutions have instilled forever into the life and work of a Jesuit.

May the Society have the courage to take up this challenge, for it is the well-spring of vigor for our life in the spirit and for our apostolic creativity.

Peter-Hans Kolvenbach, S.J.
Superior General

Rome, 1 January 1990, Solemnity of Holy Mary
Mother of God and of the Giving of the Holy Name of Jesus

FOREWORD BY FR. PEDRO ARRUPE
TO THE 1978 EDITION

Ten years ago, following the wish of the 31st General Congregation, a booklet of *Readings from the Constitutions of the Society of Jesus* was published; and this was followed in 1975 by *Jesuit Religious Life,* a compilation recommended by the 32nd General Congregation.

In fulfilling the agreeable task of presenting this edition containing both texts, I think it is important to insist on the particular value of each of them, and to explain how they differ and how they complement each other.

The old Rules of the Summary, which have their origin in St. Ignatius's own time, were first published in 1560 by Fr. Lainez. They were significantly changed by the 3rd General Congregation, and a new edition was put out by Fr. Mercurian in 1580. It was only in 1923, by a decision of the 27th General Congregation, that it was decided that they were under the exclusive control of a General Congregation.

The 30th General Congregation, in 1957, notably increased them. The 31st General Congregation restored Fr. General's competence over the Summary and recommended that he revise it completely (d. 19, nn. 14-15). In 1967, having heard the opinion of my consultors it seemed to me more appropriate to recast the text, giving it a new structure, with the following characteristics: there would be a fuller selection of texts from the Constitutions; the extracts would follow the same order as the Constitutions themselves; they would not have the character of rules "to be observed by all," but each text would be allowed to keep the same force that it holds in the Constitutions, which are directed sometimes to all Jesuits and at other times to a special category of members, but are always intended as an inspiration to all.

Jesuit Religious Life, published three years ago, has been widely distributed, inside and outside the Society. Its origins go back to the 32nd General Congregation (d. 11, n. 54). As you know, it contains "Orientations" and "Norms and Practical Directives" from the two most recent General Congregations and also, at the express recommendation of the 32nd General Congregation, from some of my own instructions to the whole Society.

This Summary of the Constitutions should not prevent our direct access to the book of the Constitutions themselves; nor, similarly, should *Jesuit Religious Life* discourage the study of the complete and ample texts of the recent General Congregations. On the contrary, this booklet should be a stimulus to draw attention to the more important paragraphs and to complete their study with a direct reading of the sources and authentic declarations of our spirituality.

The Decrees of the General Congregations and the documents that I have published relating to them provide a new reading of the Formula and of the Constitutions, responding to the needs of the present moment.

Therefore, just as the Formula and the Constitutions have passed down to us the intimate identity of the Society, so the recent General Congregations, faithful to this charism, have striven to adapt our Institute to our own times.

All of this constitutes "our way of proceeding," in the modest phrase that St. Ignatius liked to use, our own style of living the Gospel. Along with the *Summary of the Constitutions* and *Jesuit Religious Life*, the present edition offers the *Formula of the Institute*, definitively approved by Julius III in 1550, which is not only our fundamental law in "dignity and authority" (GC31 d. 4, n. 2. 1), but is also the document which "exhibits the fundamental structure of the Society, based, with the help of grace, on Gospel principles and the experience and wisdom of our holy father Ignatius and his companions" (GC31 d. 4, n. 3. 1).

It is our obligation to deepen our knowledge of our vocation to be able to live it more intensively. "We do not easily believe that we already sufficiently know our vocation, nor are we afraid to confront the fullness of such a mission" (AR XV, 1966, p. 27).

This book should be read and meditated upon; but above all it must be the object of personal and community prayer, and it must be lived by each of us every day.

It is not enough to read and meditate on it a few times: remember that St. Ignatius recommended that the Constitutions be read every month (Const. 826), and recall the pedagogical importance that he gave to repetition. I especially commend to you its reading in your meetings, retreats, and especially in the annual Exercises.

That you may take more fruit from your reading I would ask you to keep three points in mind: 1) Be conscious that the Constitutions are a concrete way of living the Exercises. A Jesuit should live the Exercises according to the Constitutions of the Society. He is a man of the Exercises and of the Constitutions. 2) Try to project what St. Ignatius says in the Constitutions on to the concrete reality of our own time: for example, when he speaks of the priority of the means which unite the instrument with God, of the criteria for the selection of ministries, or of the union of minds and hearts. 3) Seek to discover the gospel foundation for our way of proceeding. Although the explicit quotations are very few, the implicit references and the implicit principles on which the Constitutions are based are always evangelical, and we must always discover them. This is what is done in the Foreword of the first edition of the Constitutions, where the words of St. Paul are used to present "the scope and purpose of our Constitutions":

> Our way of life demands that we be men crucified to the world and to whom the world is crucified; that we be new men, who have stripped themselves of their passions to be clothed with Christ; dead, that they may live to holiness; who, in the words of St. Paul, show themselves disciples of God in labor, in vigils, in fasting, in chastity, in knowledge, in patience, in gentleness, in the spirit of holiness, in charity that is not pretended, in the word of truth; and who with the armor of justice, to right and to left, in triumph and disgrace, through fame and humiliation, in good times and bad, journey boldly to their heavenly home, bringing others with them and helping them as much as they can, looking always to the glory of God. *(From the preface to the first edition of the Constitutions, attributed to Fr. Pedro de Ribadeneira)*

Pedro Arrupe, S.J.
Superior General

Rome, 31 July 1978
Solemnity of St. Ignatius

THE FORMULA OF THE INSTITUTE
OF THE SOCIETY OF JESUS

Approved by Julius III and Inserted in the Bull
Exposcit Debitum *(21 July 1550)*

1. Whoever desires to serve as a soldier of God beneath the banner of the cross in our Society, which we desire to be designated by the name of Jesus, and to serve the Lord alone and the Church, His spouse, under the Roman Pontiff, the vicar of Christ on earth, should, after a solemn vow of perpetual chastity, poverty, and obedience, keep what follows in mind. He is a member of a Society founded chiefly for this purpose: to strive especially for the defense and propagation of the faith and for the progress of souls in Christian life and doctrine, by means of public preaching, lectures, and any other ministration whatsoever of the word of God, and further by means of the Spiritual Exercises, the education of children and unlettered persons in Christianity, and the spiritual consolation of Christ's faithful through hearing confessions and administering the other sacraments. Moreover, he should show himself ready to reconcile the estranged, compassionately assist and serve those who are in prisons or hospitals, and indeed to perform any other works of charity, according to what will seem expedient for the glory of God and the common good. Furthermore, he should carry out all these works altogether free of charge and without accepting any salary for the labor expended in all the aforementioned activities. Still further, let

any such person take care, as long as he lives, first of all to keep before his eyes God and then the nature of this Institute which he has embraced and which is, so to speak, a pathway to God; and then let him strive with all his effort to achieve this end set before him by God—each one, however, according to the grace which the Holy Spirit has given to him and according to the particular grade of his own vocation.

2. Consequently, lest anyone should perhaps show zeal, but a zeal which is not according to knowledge, the decision about each one's grade and the selection and entire distribution of employments shall be in the power of the superior general or ordinary who at any future time is to be elected by us, or in the power of those whom this superior general may appoint under himself with that authority, in order that the proper order necessary in every well-organized community may be preserved. This superior general, with the advice of his associates, shall possess the authority to establish constitutions leading to the achievement of this end which has been proposed to us, with the majority of votes always having the right to prevail. He shall also have the authority to explain officially doubts which may arise in connection with our Institute as comprised within this Formula. The council, which must necessarily be convoked to establish or change the Constitutions and for other matters of more than ordinary importance, such as the alienation or dissolution of houses and colleges once erected, should be understood (according to the explanation in our Constitutions) to be the greater part of the entire professed Society which can be summoned without grave inconvenience by the superior general. In other matters, which are of lesser importance, the same general, aided by counsel from his brethren to the extent that he will deem fitting, shall have the full right personally to order and command whatever he judges in the Lord to pertain to the glory of God and the common good, as will be explained in the Constitutions.

3. All who make the profession in this Society should un-

derstand at the time, and furthermore keep in mind as long as they live, that this entire Society and the individual members who make their profession in it are campaigning for God under faithful obedience to His Holiness Pope Paul III and his successors in the Roman pontificate. The Gospel does indeed teach us, and we know from the orthodox faith and firmly hold, that all of Christ's faithful are subject to the Roman pontiff as their head and as the vicar of Jesus Christ. But we have judged nevertheless that the following procedure will be supremely profitable to each of us and to any others who will pronounce the same profession in the future, for the sake of our greater devotion in obedience to the Apostolic See, of greater abnegation of our own wills, and of surer direction from the Holy Spirit. In addition to that ordinary bond of the three vows, we are to be obliged by a special vow to carry out whatever the present and future Roman pontiffs may order which pertains to the progress of souls and the propagation of the faith; and to go without subterfuge or excuse and at once (as far as in us lies) to whatsoever provinces they may choose to send us—whether they are pleased to send us among the Turks or any other infidels, even those who live in the region called the Indies, or among any heretics whatever, or schismatics, or any of the faithful.

4. Therefore before those who will come to us take this burden upon their shoulders, they should ponder long and seriously, as the Lord has counseled, whether they possess among their resources enough spiritual capital to complete this tower; that is, whether the Holy Spirit who moves them is offering them so much grace that with His aid they have hope of bearing the weight of this vocation. Then, after they have enlisted through the inspiration of the Lord in this militia of Christ, they ought to be prompt in carrying out this obligation which is so great, being clad for battle day and night.

5. However, to forestall among us any ambition of such missions or provinces, or any refusal of them, all our members

should have this understanding: They should not either directly or through someone else carry on negotiations with the Roman pontiff about such missions, but leave all this care to God, and to the pope himself as God's vicar, and to the superior general of the Society. This general too, just like the rest, should not treat with the said pontiff about his own being sent or not, unless after advice from the Society.

6. All should likewise vow that in all matters which pertain to the observance of this Rule they will be obedient to the one put in charge of the Society. (He should be as qualified as possible for this office and will be elected by a majority of the votes, as will be explained in the Constitutions.) Moreover, he should possess all the authority and power over the Society which are useful for its good administration, correction, and government. He should issue the commands which he knows to be opportune for achieving the end set before him by God and the Society. In his superiorship he should be ever mindful of the kindness, meekness, and charity of Christ and of the pattern set by Peter and Paul, a norm which both he and the aforementioned council should keep constantly in view. Assuredly, too, because of the great value of good order and for the sake of the constant practice of humility which has never been sufficiently praised, the individual subjects should not only be obliged to obey the general in all matters pertaining to the Society's Institute but also to recognize and properly venerate Christ as present in him.

7. From experience we have learned that a life removed as far as possible from all infection of avarice and as like as possible to evangelical poverty is more gratifying, more undefiled, and more suitable for the edification of our fellowmen. We likewise know that our Lord Jesus Christ will supply to His servants who are seeking only the kingdom of God what is necessary for food and clothing. Therefore our members, one and all, should vow perpetual poverty in such a manner that neither the professed, either as individuals or in common, nor

any house or church of theirs can acquire any civil right to any produce, fixed revenues, or possessions or to the retention of any stable goods (except those which are proper for their own use and habitation); but they should instead be content with whatever is given them out of charity for the necessities of life.

8. However, the houses which the Lord will provide are to be dedicated to labor in His vineyard and not to the pursuit of scholastic studies; and on the other hand, it appears altogether proper that workers should be provided for that same vineyard from among the young men who are inclined to piety and capable of applying themselves to learning, in order that they may form a kind of seminary for the Society, including the professed Society. Consequently, to provide facilities for studies, the professed Society should be capable of having colleges of scholastics wherever benefactors will be moved by their devotion to build and endow them. We now petition that as soon as these colleges will have been built and endowed (but not from resources which it pertains to the Holy See to apply), they may be established through authorization from the Holy See or considered to be so established. These colleges should be capable of having fixed revenues, annuities, or possessions which are to be applied to the uses and needs of the students. The general or the Society retains the full government or superintendency over the aforementioned colleges and students; and this pertains to the choice of the rectors or governors and of the scholastics; the admission, dismissal, reception, and exclusion of the same; the enactment of statutes; the arrangement, instruction, edification, and correction of the scholastics; the manner of supplying them with food, clothing, and all the other necessary materials, and every other kind of government, control, and care. All this should be managed in such a way that neither may the students be able to abuse the aforementioned goods nor may the professed Society be able to convert them to its own uses, but may use them to provide for the needs of the scholastics. These students, moreover, should

have such intellectual ability and moral character as to give solid hope that they will be suitable for the Society's functions after their studies are completed, and that thus at length, after their progress in spirit and learning has become manifest and after sufficient testing, they can be admitted into our Society.

Since all the members should be priests, they should be obliged to recite the Divine Office according to the ordinary rite of the Church, but privately and not in common or in choir. Also, in what pertains to food, clothing, and other external things, they will follow the common and approved usage of reputable priests, so that if anything is subtracted in this regard in accordance with each one's need or desire of spiritual progress, it may be offered, as will be fitting, out of devotion and not obligation, as reasonable service of the body to God.

9.   These are the matters which we were able to explain about our profession in a kind of sketch, through the good pleasure of our previously mentioned sovereign pontiff Paul and of the Apostolic See. We have now completed this explanation, in order to give brief information both to those who ask us about our plan of life and also to those who will later follow us if, God willing, we shall ever have imitators along this path. By experience we have learned that the path has many and great difficulties connected with it. Consequently we have judged it opportune to decree that no one should be permitted to pronounce his profession in this Society unless his life and doctrine have been probed by long and exacting tests (as will be explained in the Constitutions). For in all truth this Institute requires men who are thoroughly humble and prudent in Christ as well as conspicuous in the integrity of Christian life and learning. Moreover, some persons will be admitted to become coadjutors either for spiritual or temporal concerns or to become scholastics. After sufficient probations and the time specified in the Constitutions, these too should, for their greater devotion and merit, pronounce their vows. But their vows will

not be solemn (except in the case of some who with permission from the superior general will be able to make three solemn vows of this kind because of their devotion and personal worth). Instead, they will be vows by which these persons are bound as long as the superior general thinks that they should be retained in the Society, as will be explained more fully in the Constitutions. But these coadjutors and scholastics too should be admitted into this militia of Jesus Christ only after they have been diligently examined and found suitable for that same end of the Society. And may Christ deign to be favorable to these our tender beginnings, to the glory of God the Father, to whom alone be glory and honor forever. Amen.

PART ONE

READINGS FROM THE EXAMEN
AND THE CONSTITUTIONS

THE FIRST AND GENERAL EXAMEN WHICH SHOULD BE PROPOSED TO ALL WHO REQUEST ADMISSION INTO THE SOCIETY OF JESUS

CHAPTER 1. The Institute of the Society of Jesus and the diversity of its members

[1] 1. This least congregation, which at its earliest foundation was named the Society of Jesus by the Holy See, was first approved by Pope Paul III, of happy memory, in the year 1540. Later it was confirmed by the same Holy Father in 1543 and by his successor Julius III in 1550. On other occasions too it is mentioned in different briefs and apostolic letters which grant it various favors and thereby presuppose high approval and confirmation of it.

[3] 2. The end of this Society is to devote itself with God's grace not only to the salvation and perfection of the members' own souls, but also with that same grace to labor strenuously in giving aid toward the salvation and perfection of the souls of their fellowmen.

[7] 5. In addition to the three vows mentioned, the professed Society also makes an explicit vow to the sovereign pontiff as the present or future vicar of Christ our Lord. This is a vow to go anywhere His Holiness will order, whether among the faith-

ful or the infidels, without pleading an excuse and without requesting any expenses for the journey, for the sake of matters pertaining to the worship of God and the welfare of the Christian religion.

[8] 6. In other respects, for sound reasons and with attention always paid to the greater service of God, in regard to what is exterior the manner of living is ordinary. It does not contain any regular penances or austerities which are to be practiced through obligation. But those may be taken up which each one, with the superior's approval [C], thinks likely to be more helpful for his spiritual progress, as well as those which the superiors have authority to impose upon the members for the same purpose.

[9] C. This decision will be left to the superior's judgment; and he may delegate his authority to the confessor or other persons when he thinks this expedient.

Chapter 4. *Some observances within the Society which are more important for the candidates to know*

[53] 1. The intention of the first men who bound themselves together in this Society should be explained to the candidates. Those founders' mind was that those received into it should be persons already detached from the world and determined to serve God totally, whether in one religious institute or another; and further, in conformity with this, that all those who seek admission into the Society should, before they begin to live under obedience in any house or college belonging to it, distribute all the temporal goods they might have, and renounce and dispose of those they might expect to receive. Further still, the founders' intention was that the candidates should carry out this distribution first in regard to matters of debt and obligation, if any existed (and in that case provision should be made as soon as possible). In the absence of such obligations, the candidates should make the distribution in

favor of pious and holy causes, according to the words, "He has scattered abroad and has given to the poor" (Ps. 111:9 and 2 Cor. 9:9), and according to those of Christ, "If thou wilt be perfect, go, sell all that thou hast, and give to the poor . . . and follow me" (Matt. 19:21)—thus making that distribution according to their own devotion and casting away from themselves all hope of being able to possess those goods at any time.

[61] 7. Everyone who enters the Society, following the counsel of Christ our Lord that "He who leaves father" and the rest (Matt. 19:29; Luke 18:30), should judge that he should leave his father, mother, brothers, sisters, and whatever he had in the world. Even more, he should consider as spoken to himself that statement: "He who does not hate his father and mother and even his own life, cannot be my disciple" (Luke 14:26).

Consequently he should endeavor to put aside all merely natural affection for his relatives and convert it into spiritual, by loving them only with that love which rightly ordered charity requires. He should be as one who is dead to the world and to self-love and who lives only for Christ our Lord, while having Him in place of parents, brothers, and all things.

[63] 8. For the candidate's greater progress in his spiritual life and especially for his greater lowliness and humility, he should be asked whether he will be willing to have all his errors and defects, and anything else which will be noticed or known about him, manifested to his superiors by anyone who knows them outside of confession; and further, whether he along with all the others will be willing to aid in correcting and being corrected, by manifesting one another with due love and charity, to help one another more in the spiritual life, especially when this will be requested of him by the superior who has charge of them for greater glory to God.

[81] 26. If he is pleased to remain in the Society, his food, drink, clothing, shoes, and lodging will be what is characteristic

of the poor; and he should persuade himself that it will be what is worst in the house, for his greater abnegation and spiritual progress and to arrive at a certain equality and common norm among all. For where the Society's first members have passed through these necessities and greater bodily wants, the others who come to it should endeavor, as far as they can, to reach the same point as the earlier ones, or to go farther in our Lord.

[82] 27.   Moreover, besides the other pilgrimages and probations explained above, the professed before making profession, the coadjutors before taking their vows, and (when the superior thinks it wise) the scholastics before becoming approved and pronouncing their vows with the promise mentioned above, should for the love of God our Lord beg from door to door for a period of three days at the times assigned them, thus imitating those earliest members. The purpose is that, contrary to common human opinion, they may be able in God's service and praise to humiliate themselves more and make greater spiritual progress, giving glory to His Divine Majesty. Another purpose is to enable them to find themselves more disposed to do the same begging when they are so commanded, or when it is expedient or necessary for them as they travel through various regions of the world, according to what the supreme vicar of Christ our Lord may order or assign to them, or, in his place, the one who will find himself superior of the Society. For our profession requires that we be prepared and very much ready for whatever is enjoined upon us in our Lord and at whatsoever time, without asking for or expecting any reward in this present and transitory life, but hoping always for that life which in its entirety is eternal, through God's supreme mercy.

[83] 28.   But to come down to details, during the tests of humility and abnegation of oneself through the performance of lowly and humble tasks, such as working in the kitchen, cleaning the house, and all the rest of these services, one

should take on more promptly those in which greater repugnance is found, if one has been ordered to do them.

[84] 29. When anyone begins to perform the services of the kitchen or to aid the cook, with great humility he must obey in all things pertaining to his office, by showing him always complete obedience. For if he should not do this, neither, it seems, would he show obedience to any other superior, since genuine obedience considers, not the person to whom it is offered, but Him for whose sake it is offered; and if it is exercised for the sake of our Creator and Lord alone, then it is the very Lord of everything who is obeyed. In no manner, therefore, ought one to consider whether he who gives the order is the cook of the house or its superior, or one person rather than another. For, to consider the matter with sound understanding, obedience is not shown either to these persons or for their sake, but to God alone and only for the sake of God our Creator and Lord.

[89] 32. In time of illness one ought to observe obedience of great integrity not only toward his spiritual superiors that they may direct his soul, but also and with equal humility toward the physicians and infirmarians that they may care for his body; for the former work for his complete spiritual welfare and the latter for that which is corporal. Furthermore, the one who is sick should, by showing his great humility and patience, endeavor to give no less edification in the time of his illness to those who visit him and converse and deal with him than he does in the time of full health, for the greater glory to God.

[91] 34. Through reflection in our Lord, what follows has seemed good to us in His Divine Majesty. It is a matter of great and even extraordinary importance that the superiors should have a complete understanding of the subjects, that by means of it they may be able to direct and govern them better, and while looking out for the subjects' interests guide them better into the paths of the Lord.

[92] 35. Likewise, the more completely the superiors know these subjects' interior and exterior affairs, just so much the better will they be able, with greater diligence, love, and care, to help the subjects and to guard their souls from various inconveniences and dangers which might occur later on. Further still, in conformity with our profession and manner of proceeding, we should always be ready to travel about in various regions of the world, on all occasions when the supreme pontiff or our immediate superior orders us. To proceed without error in such missions, or in sending some persons and not others, or some for one task and others for different ones, it is not only highly but even supremely important for the superior to have complete knowledge of the inclinations and motions of those who are in his charge, and to what defects or sins they have been or are more moved and inclined; that thus he may direct them better, without exposing them beyond the measure of their capacity to dangers or labors greater than they could in our Lord endure with a spirit of love; and also that the superior, while keeping to himself what he learns in secret, may be better able to organize and arrange what is expedient for the whole body of the Society.

[101] 44. It is likewise highly important to bring this to the mind of those who are being examined (through their esteeming it highly and pondering it in the sight of our Creator and Lord), to how great a degree it helps and profits one in the spiritual life to abhor in its totality and not in part whatever the world loves and embraces, and to accept and desire with all possible energy whatever Christ our Lord has loved and embraced. Just as the men of the world who follow the world love and seek with such great diligence honors, fame, and esteem for a great name on earth, as the world teaches them, so those who are progressing in the spiritual life and truly following Christ our Lord love and intensely desire everything opposite. That is to say, they desire to clothe themselves with the same clothing and uniform of their Lord because of the

love and reverence which He deserves, to such an extent that where there would be no offense to His Divine Majesty and no imputation of sin to the neighbor, they would wish to suffer injuries, false accusations, and affronts, and to be held and esteemed as fools (but without their giving any occasion for this), because of their desire to resemble and imitate in some manner our Creator and Lord Jesus Christ, by putting on His clothing and uniform, since it was for our spiritual profit that He clothed Himself as He did. For He gave us an example that in all things possible to us we might seek, through the aid of His grace, to imitate and follow Him, since He is the way which leads men to life. Therefore the candidate should be asked whether he finds himself in a state of desires like these which are so salutary and fruitful for the perfection of his soul.

[102] 45. In a case where through human weakness and personal misery the candidate does not experience in himself such ardent desires in our Lord, he should be asked whether he has any desires to experience them. If he answers affirmatively that he does wish to have holy desires of this kind, then, that he may the better reach them in fact, he should be questioned further: Is he determined and ready to accept and suffer with patience, through the help of God's grace, any such injuries, mockeries, and affronts entailed by the wearing of this uniform of Christ our Lord, and any other affronts offered him, whether by someone inside the house or the Society (where he desires to obey, be humiliated, and gain eternal life) or outside it by any persons whatsoever on earth, while returning them not evil for evil but good for evil?

[103] 46. The better to arrive at this degree of perfection which is so precious in the spiritual life, his chief and most earnest endeavor should be to seek in our Lord his greater abnegation and continual mortification in all things possible; and our endeavor should be to help him in those things to the extent that our Lord gives us His grace, for His greater praise and glory.

THE CONSTITUTIONS OF THE SOCIETY OF JESUS

Preamble to the Constitutions

[134] 1.   Although it must be the Supreme Wisdom and Goodness of God our Creator and Lord which will preserve, direct, and carry forward in His divine service this least Society of Jesus, just as He deigned to begin it; and although what helps most on our own part toward this end must be, more than any exterior constitutions, the interior law of charity and love which the Holy Spirit writes and engraves upon hearts; nevertheless, since the gentle arrangement of Divine Providence requires cooperation from His creatures, and since too the Vicar of Christ our Lord has ordered this, and since the examples given by the saints and reason itself teach us so in our Lord, we think it necessary that constitutions should be written to aid us to proceed better, in conformity with our Institute, along the path of divine service on which we have entered.

PART I. THE ADMISSION TO PROBATION

CHAPTER 1. The person who admits

[142] 3.   It is highly important for the divine service to make a proper selection of those who are admitted and to take care to know their abilities and vocation well.

[143] 4. Both he who has the authority to admit and his helper ought to know the Society's concerns and to be zealous for its good progress, so that no other consideration will be so strong as to deter him from what he judges in our Lord to be more suitable for His divine service in this Society. Therefore he should be very moderate in his desire to admit [C].

[144] C. Just as care should be taken to cooperate with the divine motion and vocation by endeavoring to secure in the Society an increase of workers for the holy vineyard of Christ our Lord, so too should much thought be given to admit only those who possess the qualifications required for this Institute, for the divine glory.

CHAPTER 2. *The candidates who should be admitted*

[147] 1. To speak in general of those who should be admitted, the greater the number of natural and infused gifts someone has from God our Lord which are useful for what the Society aims at in His divine service, and the more experience the candidate has in the use of these gifts, the more suitable will he be for reception into the Society.

[152] 4. In view of the end of our Institute and our manner of proceeding, we are convinced in our Lord that to admit persons who are very difficult or unserviceable to the congregation is not conducive to His greater service and praise, even though their admission would be useful to themselves.

[161] 13. The extrinsic gifts of nobility, wealth, reputation, and the like, are not necessary when the others are present, just as they do not suffice if those others are lacking. But to the extent that they aid toward edification, they render more fit to be admitted those who would be fit without them because they have the other qualifications mentioned above. The more an applicant is distinguished for those qualifications the more suitable will he be for this Society unto glory of God our Lord,

and the less he is distinguished by them, the less suitable. But the holy unction of the Divine Wisdom will teach the mean which should be retained in all this to those who have charge of that matter, which was undertaken for his greater service and praise.

CHAPTER 3. *The impediments to admission*

[163] 1. The charity and zeal for souls in which this Society exerts itself according to the purpose of its Institute embrace all kinds of persons, to serve and help them in the Lord of all men to attain to beatitude. Nevertheless, when there is a question of incorporating persons into the same Society, that charity and zeal should embrace only those who are judged useful for the end it seeks (as has been said).

PART II. THE DISMISSAL OF THOSE WHO WERE ADMITTED BUT DID NOT PROVE THEMSELVES FIT

CHAPTER 1. *Who can be dismissed, and by whom*

[204] 1. Just as it is proper, for the sake of the end sought in this Society, the service of God our Lord by helping souls who are His, to preserve and multiply the workers who are found fit and useful for carrying this work forward, so is it also expedient to dismiss those who are found unsuitable, and who as time passes make it evident that this is not their vocation or that their remaining in the Society does not advance the common good. However, just as excessive readiness should not be had in admitting candidates, so ought it to be used even less in dismissing them; instead, one ought to proceed with much consideration and weighing in our Lord. The more fully one has been incorporated into the Society, the more serious ought the reasons to be. Nevertheless, no matter how advanced the

incorporation may be, in some cases anyone can and should be separated from the Society.

[206] 2. The authority to dismiss will be vested chiefly in the Society as a whole when it is assembled in a general congregation. The superior general will have the same authority in all other cases except one involving himself. The other members of the Society participate, each one, in this authority to the extent that it is communicated to them by the head.

CHAPTER 2. *The causes for dismissal*

[209] 1. The discreet charity[1] of the superior who has the authority to dismiss ought to ponder before God our Lord the causes which suffice for dismissal. But to speak in general, they seem to be of four kinds.

[210] 2. The first cause is present if it is perceived[2] in the same Lord of ours that someone's remaining in this Society would be contrary to His honor and glory, because this person

---

[1] Not infrequently in the Constitutions, St. Ignatius insists on *discreet charity*, a fundamental and critical reality which ought to govern all full observance of the Constitutions, above all on the part of the superiors when they are making decisions to do with government. The letter of the Constitutions does not dispense the superior from *discreet charity;* rather it is imposed upon him. What we have is the point of convergence between the eternal love of God and the judgment of the spiritual man. This convergence points at one and the same time to a charity which is full of insight and judgment, and to a discernment and a choice which are inspired and directed by love, a love which itself achieves the discernment and which comes from the Spirit of love. This is what Paul is asking for on behalf of the Philippians: "That your love may grow ever richer and richer in knowledge and insight of every kind, and may thus bring you the gift of true discrimination." (Phil. 1:9-10)

[2] The word *sentir* is characteristic of the vocabulary of Ignatius, and it has been given different interpretations by various illustrious scholars. We meet it here in the context of election or, more precisely, of spiritual discernment. It signifies the spiritual sensitivity of a man, his receptivity and interior reaction which complement his use of his rational knowledge. Together they permit a man to arrive where God wishes to lead him.

is judged to be incorrigible in some passions or vices which offend His Divine Majesty. The more serious and culpable these are, the less ought they to be tolerated, even though they do not scandalize the others because they are occult.

[212] 3. The second cause is present if it is perceived in the same Lord that to retain someone would be contrary to the good of the Society. Since this is a universal good, it ought to be preferred to the good of one individual by one who is sincerely seeking the divine service. This cause would be present if in the course of the probation some impediments or notable defects should be discovered which the applicant failed to mention earlier during the examination, or if experience should show that he would be highly unprofitable and hinder rather than aid the Society, because of his notable incompetency for any office whatever.

[216] 4. The third cause is present if one's remaining is seen to be simultaneously contrary to the good of the Society and of the individual. For example, this could arise from the body, if during the probation such illnesses and weakness are observed in someone that it seems in our Lord that he could not carry on the labor which is required in our manner of proceeding in order to serve God our Lord by that way. It could also arise from the soul, if the one who was admitted to probation is unable to bring himself to live under obedience and to adapt himself to the Society's manner of proceeding, because he is unable or does not wish to submit his own judgment, or because he has other obstacles arising from nature or habits.

[217] 5. The fourth cause is present if his remaining is seen to be contrary to the good of others outside the Society. This could arise from discovery of the bond of marriage, or of legitimate slavery, or of debts of importance, after he concealed the truth about this matter in the examination.

If any one whatsoever of these four causes exists, it seems that God our Lord will be better served by giving the person proper dismissal than by employing indiscreet charity in retaining him in whom the causes are found.

CHAPTER 3. *The manner of dismissing*

[218] 1. With those who must be dismissed, that manner ought to be employed which before God our Lord is likely to give greater satisfaction to the one who dismisses as well as to the one dismissed and to the others within and without the house.

PART III. THE PRESERVATION AND PROGRESS OF THOSE WHO ARE IN PROBATION

CHAPTER 1. *Preservation pertaining to the soul and to progress in virtues*

[243] 1. Due consideration and prudent care should be employed toward preserving in their vocation those who are being kept and tested in the houses or colleges, and toward enabling them to make progress, both in spirit and in virtues along the path of the divine service, in such a manner that there is also proper care for the health and bodily strength necessary to labor in the Lord's vineyard.

[244] 2. In regard to the soul, it is of great importance to keep those who are in probation away from all imperfections and from whatever can impede their greater spiritual progress.

[250] 4. All should take special care to guard with great diligence the gates of their senses (especially the eyes, ears, and tongue) from all disorder, to preserve themselves in peace and true humility of their souls, and to give an indication of it by silence when it should be kept and, when they must speak, by the discretion and edification of their words, the modesty of

their countenance, the maturity of their walk, and all their movements, without giving any sign of impatience or pride. In everything they should try and desire to give the advantage to the others, esteeming them all in their hearts as better than themselves (Phil. 2:3) and showing exteriorly, in an unassuming and simple religious manner, the respect and reverence befitting each one's state, in such a manner that by observing one another they may grow in devotion and praise God our Lord, whom each one should endeavor to recognize in his neighbor as in His image.

[251] 5. In the refection of the body care should be taken to observe temperance, decorum, and propriety both interior and exterior in everything. A blessing should precede the meal and a thanksgiving come after it; and all ought to recite these with proper devotion and reverence.

[253] 6. Generally, all those who are in good health should be engaged in spiritual or exterior occupations. Furthermore, just as those who perform duties should be given alleviation if they need it, so when they have time left over they should occupy themselves in other things, that idleness, which is the source of all evils, may have no place in the house, as far as this is possible.

[254] 7. That they may begin to experience the virtue of holy poverty, all should be taught that they should not have the use of anything of their own as being their own.

[257] 8. Likewise they should understand that they may not lend, borrow, or dispose of anything in the house unless the superior knows it and consents.

[258] 9. If someone upon entering or after placing himself under obedience should find devotion in disposing of his temporal goods or a part of them in favor of the Society, it is beyond any doubt a matter of greater perfection, self-dispossession, and abnegation of all self-love, not to single out particular places with fond affection, or through that affection to apply

his goods to one place rather than to another. Rather, he does better if, while desiring the greater and more universal good of the Society (which is directed to greater divine service and greater universal good and spiritual progress of souls), he leaves to him who has charge of the whole Society this judgment as to whether the goods ought to be applied to one place rather than to another of that same province.

[260] 10. They should be taught how to guard themselves from the illusions of the devil in their devotions and how to defend themselves from all temptations. They should know the means which can be found to overcome them and to apply themselves to the pursuit of the true and solid virtues, whether this be with many spiritual visitations or with fewer, by endeavoring always to go forward in the path of the divine service.

[261] 11. They should practice the daily examination of their consciences and confess and receive Communion at least every eight days, unless the superior for some reason orders otherwise. There should be one confessor for all, assigned by him who has charge of the others. Or if this is impossible, everyone should at least have his own regular confessor to whom he should keep his conscience completely open, and who should be informed about the cases which the superior reserves to himself. These cases will be those where it appears necessary or highly expedient for the superior to have knowledge, that he may the better provide remedies and protect from difficulties those whom he has in his charge.

[263] 12. It will be beneficial to have a faithful and competent person whose function is to instruct and teach the novices in regard to their interior and exterior conduct, to encourage them toward this correct deportment, to remind them of it, and to give them kindly admonition; a person whom all those who are in probation may love and to whom they may have recourse in their temptations and open themselves with confidence, hoping to receive from him in our Lord counsel and aid in everything.

They should be advised, too, that they ought not to keep secret any temptation which they do not tell to him or their confessor or the superior, being happy that their entire soul is completely open to them. Moreover, they will tell him not only their defects but also their penances or mortifications, or their devotions and all their virtues, with a pure desire to be directed if in anything they have gone astray, and without desiring to be guided by their own judgment unless it agrees with the opinion of him whom they have in place of Christ our Lord.

[265] 13. Temptations ought to be anticipated by their opposites, for example, if someone is observed to be inclined toward pride, by exercising him in lowly matters thought fit to aid toward humbling him; and similarly of other evil inclinations.

[269] 15. In regard to the corrections and penances, the measure which ought to be observed will be left to the discreet charity of the superior and of those whom he has delegated in his place, that they may adjust them in accordance with the disposition of the persons and with the edification of each and every one of them for divine glory. Each one ought to accept them in a good spirit with a genuine desire of his emendation and spiritual profit, even when the reason for their imposition is not that of some blameworthy defect.

[272] 17. In their illnesses all should try to draw fruit from them not only for themselves but for the edification of others. They should not be impatient nor difficult to please. Rather, they should have and show much patience and obedience to the physician and infirmarian, and employ good and edifying words which show that the sickness is accepted as a gift from the hand of our Creator and Lord, since it is a gift not less than is health.

[273] 18. As far as possible, we should all think alike and speak alike, in conformity with the Apostle's teaching; and differing doctrines ought not to be permitted, either orally in

sermons or public lectures, or in books; (and it will not be permissible to publish books without the approval and permission of the superior general, who will entrust the examination of them to at least three persons of sound doctrine and clear judgment about the field in question). Even in regard to things which are to be done, diversity, which is generally the mother of discord and the enemy of union of wills, should be avoided as far as possible. This union and agreement among them all ought to be sought with great care and the opposite ought not to be permitted, in order that, being united among themselves by the bond of fraternal charity, they may be able better and more efficaciously to apply themselves in the service of God and the aid of their fellowmen.

[277] 20. On certain days of each week instruction should be given about Christian doctrine, the manner of making a good and fruitful confession, receiving Communion, assisting at Mass and serving it, praying, meditating, and reading [good spiritual books], in accordance with each one's capacity. Likewise, care should be taken that they learn what is proper and do not let it be forgotten, and put it into practice; that is, all of them should give time to spiritual things and strive to acquire as much devotion as divine grace imparts to them. Toward this purpose it will help to give some of the Spiritual Exercises, or all of them, to those who have not made them, according to what is judged expedient for them in our Lord.

[282] 22. It will be very specially helpful to perform with all possible devotion the tasks in which humility and charity are practiced more; and, to speak in general, the more one binds himself to God our Lord and shows himself more generous toward His Divine Majesty, the more will he find God more generous toward himself and the more disposed will he be to receive graces and spiritual gifts which are greater each day.

[284] 23. To make progress, it is very expedient and highly necessary that all should devote themselves to complete obedience, by recognizing the superior, whoever he is, as being

in the place of Christ our Lord and by maintaining interior reverence and love for him. They should obey entirely and promptly, not only by exterior execution of what the superior commands, with becoming energy and humility, and without excuses and murmurings even though things are commanded which are difficult and repugnant to sensitive nature [V]; but they should try to maintain in their inmost souls genuine resignation and true abnegation of their own wills and judgments, by bringing their wills and judgments wholly into conformity with what the superior wills and judges, in all things in which no sin is seen, and by regarding the superior's will and judgment as the rule of their own, in order to conform themselves more completely to the first and supreme rule of all good will and judgment, which is the Eternal Goodness and Wisdom.

[285] V. It will be helpful from time to time for superiors to see to it that those who are in probation feel their obedience and poverty, by testing them for their greater spiritual progress in the manner in which God tested Abraham, and that they may give an example of their virtue and grow in it. But in this the superiors should as far as possible observe the measure and proportion of what each can bear, as discretion will dictate.

[286] 24. That they may exercise themselves more in obedience, it is good and likewise highly necessary that they should obey not only the superior of the Society or house, but also the subordinate officials who hold their authority from him, in regard to everything for which that authority over them was given. They should accustom themselves to consider not who the person is whom they obey, but rather who He is for whose sake they obey and whom they obey in all, who is Christ our Lord.

[287] 25. All should love poverty as a mother, and according to the measure of holy discretion all should, when occasions arise, feel some effects of it. Further, as is stated in the Examen, after the first year they should be ready, each one, to dispose

of their temporal goods whenever the superior may command it, in the manner which was explained to them in the afore-mentioned Examen.

[288] 26. All should make diligent efforts to keep their intention right, not only in regard to their state of life but also in all particular details. In these they should always aim at serving and pleasing the Divine Goodness for its own sake and because of the incomparable love and benefits with which God has anticipated us, rather than for fear of punishments or hope of rewards, although they ought to draw help also from them. Further, they should often be exhorted to seek God our Lord in all things, stripping off from themselves the love of creatures to the extent that this is possible, in order to turn their love upon the Creator of them, by loving Him in all creatures and all of them in Him, in conformity with His holy and divine will.

CHAPTER 2. *The preservation of the body*

[292] 1. Just as an excessive preoccupation over the needs of the body is blameworthy, so too a proper concern about the preservation of one's health and bodily strength for the divine service is praiseworthy, and all should exercise it. Consequently, when they perceive that something is harmful to them or that something else is necessary in regard to their diet, cloth-ing, living quarters, office or the manner of carrying it out, and similarly of other matters, all ought to inform the superior about it or the one whom he appoints. But meanwhile they should observe two things. First, before informing him, they should recollect themselves to pray, and after this, if they perceive that they ought to represent the matter to him who is in charge, they should do it. Second, after they have repre-sented it by word of mouth or by a short note as a precaution against his forgetting it, they should leave the whole care of the matter to him and regard what he ordains as better,

without arguing or insisting upon it either themselves or through another, whether he grants the request or not [A]. For the subject must persuade himself that what the superior decides after being informed is more suitable for the divine service and the subject's own greater good in our Lord.

[293] A. Even though the subject who represents his need ought not personally to argue or urge the matter, nevertheless if the superior has not yet understood it, and if he requests further explanation, the subject will give it. If by chance the superior forgets to provide after he has indicated his intention to do so, it is not out of order to recall it to his memory or to represent it with becoming modesty.

[294] 2. There should be a proper order, as far as may be possible, for the time of eating, sleeping, and rising, and ordinarily all should observe it.

[300] 5. The chastisement of the body ought not to be immoderate or indiscreet in abstinences, vigils, and other external penances and labors which damage and impede greater goods. Therefore it is expedient for each one to keep his confessor informed of what he does in this matter. If the confessor thinks that there is excess or has a doubt, he should refer the matter to the superior. All this is done that the procedure may be attended by greater light and God our Lord may be more glorified through our souls and bodies.

PART IV.   THE INSTRUCTION OF THOSE WHO ARE RETAINED IN THE SOCIETY, IN LEARNING AND IN OTHER MEANS OF HELPING THEIR FELLOWMEN

Preamble

[308] A.   The aim and end of this Society is, by traveling through the various regions of the world at the order of the supreme vicar of Christ our Lord or of the superior of the Society itself, to preach, hear confessions, and use all the other means it can with the grace of God to help souls. Consequently it has seemed necessary to us, or at least highly expedient, that those who will enter the Society should be persons of good life and sufficient learning for the aforementioned work. But in comparison with others, those who are both good and learned are few; and even among those few, most of them already seek rest from their previous labors. As a result, the increase of the Society from such men of letters who are both good and learned is, we find, something very difficult to achieve, because of the great labors and the great abnegation of oneself which are required in the Society.

Therefore all of us, desiring to preserve and develop the Society for greater glory and service to God our Lord, have thought it wise to proceed by another path. That is, our procedure will be to admit young men who because of their good habits of life and ability give hope that they will become both virtuous and learned in order to labor in the vineyard of Christ our Lord.

CHAPTER 4.   The care and welfare of the scholastics admitted

[339] 1. What was stated in Part III will suffice about the care and welfare, in regard to the body and external matters, of those who live in the colleges. That is, special attention should

be given to their abstaining from studies at times inopportune for bodily health, to their taking sufficient sleep, and to their observance of moderation in mental labors, that they may have greater endurance in them both during the years of study and later on in using what they have studied for the glory of God our Lord.

[340] 2. In regard to spiritual matters, the same order or procedure will be used with those who are received in the colleges, as long as they are still going through probations, as that which is observed with those who are received in the houses. But after they have been approved and while they are applying themselves to their studies, just as care must be taken that through fervor in study they do not grow cool in their love of true virtues and of religious life, so also during that time there will not be much place for mortifications and long prayers and meditations. For their devoting themselves to learning, which they acquire with a pure intention of serving God and which in a certain way requires the whole man, will be not less but rather more pleasing to God our Lord during this time of study.

[346] 5. For greater devotion, and to refresh the memory of the obligation they are under, and to confirm themselves more solidly in their vocation, it will be good for the scholastics twice each year to renew their simple vows, which will be treated in Part V.

CHAPTER 6.   Means by which the scholastics will progress toward learning the aforementioned branches well

[360] 1. In order to make great progress in these branches, the scholastics should strive first of all to keep their souls pure and their intention in studying right, by seeking in their studies nothing except the glory of God and the good of souls. Moreover, they should frequently beg in prayer for grace to make progress in learning for the sake of this end.

[361] 2. Furthermore, they should keep their resolution firm to be thoroughly genuine and earnest students, by persuading themselves that while they are in the colleges they cannot do anything more pleasing to God our Lord than to study with the intention mentioned above; likewise, that even if they never have occasion to employ the matter studied, their very labor in studying, taken up as it ought to be because of charity and obedience, is itself work highly meritorious in the sight of the Divine and Supreme Majesty.

[362] 3. The impediments which distract from study should also be removed, both those arising from devotions and mortifications which are too numerous or without proper order and also those springing from their cares and exterior occupations whether in duties inside the house or outside it in conversations, confessions, and other activities with one's fellowmen, as far as it is possible in our Lord to excuse oneself from them. For in order that the scholastics may be able to help their fellowmen better later on by what they have learned, it is wise to postpone exercises such as these, pious though they are, until after the years of study, since there will be others to attend to them in the meantime. All this should be done with a greater intention of service and divine glory.

CHAPTER 8. *The instruction of the scholastics in the means of helping their fellowmen*

[400] 1. In view of the objective which the Society seeks by means of its studies, toward the end of them it is good for the scholastics to begin to accustom themselves to the spiritual arms which they must employ in aiding their fellowmen; and this work can be begun in the colleges, even though it is more properly and extensively done in the houses.

[401] 2. First of all, those who in the judgment of the superior should be ordained are to be taught how to say Mass not only with interior understanding and devotion but also

with an exterior manner good for the edification of those who hear the Mass. All the members of the Society should as far as possible use the same uniform ceremonies, by conforming themselves in them, as far as the diversity of regions permits, to the Roman usage as the one which is more universal and embraced in a special way by the Apostolic See.

[402] 3. Similarly, they will exercise themselves in preaching and in delivering sacred lectures in a manner suitable for the edification of the people, which is different from the scholastic manner, by endeavoring to learn the vernacular language well, to have, as matters previously studied and ready at hand, the means which are more useful for this ministry, and to avail themselves of all appropriate means to perform it better and with greater fruit for souls.

[406] 4. They should also practice themselves in the administration of the sacraments of confession and Communion, by keeping fresh in mind and endeavoring to put into practice not merely what pertains to themselves, but also what pertains to the penitents and communicants, that they may receive and frequent these sacraments well and fruitfully for divine glory.

[408] 5. After they have had experience of the Spiritual Exercises in their own selves, they should acquire experience in giving them to others. Each one should know how to give an explanation of them and how to employ this spiritual weapon, since it is obvious that God our Lord has made it so effective for His service [E].

[409] E. They could begin by giving the Exercises to some in whose cases less is risked, and by conferring about their method of procedure with someone more experienced, noting well what he finds more useful and what less so. Their explanation of the Exercises should be given in such a manner that it does not merely give satisfaction to the others but also moves them to desire to be helped by the Exercises. Generally, only the exercises of the first week should be given. When they

are given in their entirety, this should be done with outstanding persons or with those who desire to decide upon their state of life.

[410] 6. They should likewise bestow appropriate study upon the method of teaching Christian doctrine and of adapting themselves to the capacities of children or simple persons.

[412] 7. Just as one's fellowmen are helped to live well by what has been stated above, so an effort should be made to know what helps them to die well and what procedure should be used at a moment so important for gaining or losing the ultimate end, eternal happiness.

[414] 8. In general, they ought to be instructed about the manner of acting proper to a member of the Society, who has to associate with so great a diversity of persons throughout such varied regions. Hence they should foresee the inconveniences which may arise and the opportunities which can be grasped for the greater service of God, by using some means at one time and others at another. Although all this can be taught only by the unction of the Holy Spirit and by the prudence which God our Lord communicates to those who trust in His Divine Majesty, nevertheless the way can at least be opened by some suggestions which aid and dispose one for the effect which must be produced by divine grace.

CHAPTER 10. *The government of the colleges*

[423] 4. Care should be taken that the rector be a man of great example, edification, and mortification of all his evil inclinations, and one especially approved in regard to his obedience and humility. He ought likewise to be discreet, fit for governing, experienced both in matters of business and of the spiritual life. He should know how to mingle severity with kindness at the proper times. He should be solicitous, stalwart under work, a man of learning, and finally, one in whom the

higher superiors can confide and to whom they can with security delegate their authority. For the greater this delegated authority will be, the better will the colleges be governed for greater divine glory.

[424] 5. The function of the rector will be first of all to sustain the whole college by his prayer and holy desires, and then to bring it about that the Constitutions are observed [B]. He should watch over all his subjects with great care, and guard them against difficulties from within or without the house by anticipating the difficulties and remedying them if they have occurred, in the way that seems conducive to the good of the individuals and to that of all. He should strive to promote their progress in virtues and learning, and care for their health and for the temporal goods both stable and movable. He should appoint officials discreetly, observe how they proceed, and retain them in office or change them as he judges appropriate in the Lord. In general he ought to see to it that what has been stated about the colleges in the preceding chapters is carried out.

He should observe in its entirety the submission he ought to maintain not merely toward the superior general but also to the provincial superior, by keeping him informed and having recourse to him in the matters of greater moment, and by following the order given him, since the provincial is his superior, in the same way as those of his own college should act toward him. His subjects ought to hold him in great respect and reverence as one who holds the place of Christ our Lord, while leaving to him with true obedience the free disposal of themselves and their affairs, not keeping anything closed to him, not even their own conscience. Rather, as has been stated in the Examen, they should manifest their conscience to him at fixed times, and more frequently when there is reason, without showing any repugnance or any manifestations of contrary opinion, that by the union of their opinion and will with his and by proper submission they may be better preserved and make greater progress in the divine service.

[425] B. Thus, just as it will pertain to the rector to endeavor to have the Constitutions observed in their entirety, so it will be his to grant dispensations from them with authority from his own superiors, when he judges that such would be the intention of the one who composed them, in a particular case according to occurrences and necessities and while keeping his attention fixed on the greater common good.

[434] 8. The rector should endeavor that all those in the colleges practice an integral obedience to each official in his own office, and these officials to the minister and to the rector himself, in accordance with the order which he prescribes to them. Ordinarily those who have charge of others who must obey them ought to give them an example by the obedience which they themselves observe to their own superiors as persons holding the place of Christ our Lord.

[435] 9. A suitable order of time for study, prayer, Masses, lectures, eating and sleeping, and so on will be helpful for everything. Thus a signal will be given at designated times. When it is heard, all should go immediately, leaving even a letter they have begun. When these hours ought to be changed because of the seasons or other unusual reasons, the rector or the one in charge should consider the matter and what he orders should be observed.

PART V. ADMISSION OR INCORPORATION INTO THE SOCIETY

CHAPTER 1. Admission, who should admit, and when

[510] 1. Those who have been tested in the Society sufficiently and for a time long enough that both parties may know whether their remaining in it is conducive to greater service

and glory to God our Lord, ought to be admitted, not to probation as was the case in the beginning, but in a more intrinsic manner as members of one same body of the Society [A].

[511] A. The Society, when we speak in the most comprehensive sense of the term, includes all those who live under obedience to its superior general. Thus it comprises even the novices and the persons who, desiring to live and die in the Society, are in probation to be admitted into it under one of the other categories of membership about to be described.

No matter in which one of these four categories one finds himself in our Society, he is capable of sharing in the spiritual favors which, according to the grant of the Apostolic See, the superior general may dispense in the Society for greater glory to God.

CHAPTER 2. *The qualities of those to be admitted*

[516] 1.   No one should be admitted unless he has been judged fit in our Lord; for admission to profession those persons will be judged worthy whose life is well-known through long and thorough probations and is approved by the superior general, to whom a report will be sent by the other superiors or others from whom the general desires information.

For this purpose, after those who were sent to studies have achieved the diligent and careful formation of the intellect by learning, they will find it helpful during the period of the last probation to apply themselves in the school of the heart, by exercising themselves in spiritual and corporal pursuits which can engender in them greater humility, abnegation of all sensual love and will and judgment of their own, and also greater knowledge and love of God our Lord; that when they themselves have made progress they can better help others to progress for glory to God our Lord.

[520] 3. In addition to these, some can be admitted to the profession of only three solemn vows. But this will be done rarely and for special and important reasons. These members should have been known in the Society, giving in it great satisfaction by their talent and virtues, for glory to God our Lord.

[522] 4. To be admitted among the formed coadjutors, a subject should likewise have given satisfaction in regard to his life and good example and his ability to aid the Society, either in spiritual matters by his learning or in exterior matters without the learning, each one according to what God has communicated to him. By his discretion the superior general will have to appraise this matter too, unless it seems good to him to entrust it to the particular persons in whom he has much confidence in our Lord.

[523] 5. That subjects may be admitted among the approved scholastics, proportionately the same set of requirements remains. Especially in regard to their ability, there should be hope that they will succeed in their studies, in the judgment of the general or of the one whom he designates while confiding in the discretion and goodness which God our Lord has given to him.

PART VI. THE PERSONAL LIFE OF THOSE ALREADY ADMITTED OR INCORPORATED INTO THE SOCIETY

CHAPTER 1. What pertains to obedience

[547] 1. In order that those already admitted to profession or to membership among the formed coadjutors may be able to apply themselves more fruitfully according to our Institute in the service of God and the aid of their fellowmen, they themselves ought to observe certain things.

What pertains to the vow of chastity does not require explanation, since it is evident how perfectly it should be preserved through the endeavor in this matter to imitate the angelic purity by the purity of the body and mind. Therefore, with this presupposed, we shall now treat of holy obedience.

All should keep their resolution firm to observe obedience and to distinguish themselves in it, not only in the matters of obligation but also in the others, even though nothing else is perceived except the indication of the superior's will without an expressed command. They should keep in view God our Creator and Lord, for whom such obedience is practiced, and they should endeavor to proceed in a spirit of love and not as men troubled by fear. Hence all of us should exert ourselves not to miss any point of perfection which we can with God's grace attain in the observance of all the Constitutions [A] and in our manner of proceeding in our Lord, by applying all our energies with very special care to the virtue of obedience shown first to the sovereign pontiff and then to the superiors of the Society.

Consequently, in all the things into which obedience can with charity be extended [B], we should be ready to receive its command just as if it were coming from Christ our Savior, since we are practicing the obedience to one in His place and because of love and reverence for Him. Therefore we should be ready to leave unfinished any letter or anything else of ours which has been begun and to apply our whole mind and all the energy we have in the Lord of all that our obedience may be perfect in every detail [C], in regard to the execution, the willing, and the understanding. We should perform with great alacrity, spiritual joy, and perseverance whatever has been commanded to us, persuading ourselves that everything is just and renouncing with blind obedience any contrary opinion and judgment of our own in all things which the superior commands and in which (as it was stated) some species of sin cannot be judged to be present. We ought to be firmly convinced that everyone of those who live under obedience ought to allow himself to be carried and directed by Divine Providence through the agency of the superior as if he were a lifeless body which allows itself to be carried to any place and to be treated in any manner desired, or as if he were an old man's staff which serves in any place and in any manner whatsoever in which the holder wishes to use it. For in this way the obedient man ought joyfully to devote himself to any task whatsoever in which the superior desires to employ him to aid the whole body of the religious Institute; and he ought to hold it as certain that by this procedure he is conforming himself with the divine will more than by anything else he could do while following his own will and different judgment.

[548] A. These first Declarations which are published along with the Constitutions bind with the same authority as the Constitutions. Therefore in the observance, equal care should be bestowed upon the Declarations and the Constitutions.

[549] B. Such things are all those in which some sin is not manifest.

[550] C. The command of obedience is fulfilled in regard to the execution when the thing commanded is done; in regard to the willing when the one who obeys wills the same thing as the one who commands; in regard to the understanding when he forms the same judgment as the one commanding and regards what he is commanded as good. And that obedience is imperfect in which there does not exist, in addition to the execution, also that agreement in willing and judging between him who commands and him who obeys.

[551] 2. Likewise, it should be strongly recommended to all that they should have and show great reverence, especially interior reverence, to their superiors, by considering and reverencing Jesus Christ in them; and from their hearts they should warmly love their superiors as fathers in Him. Thus in everything they should proceed in a spirit of charity, keeping

nothing exterior or interior hidden from the superiors and desiring them to be informed about everything, in order that the superiors may be the better able to direct them in everything along the path of salvation and perfection. For that reason, once a year and as many times more as their superior thinks good, all the professed and formed coadjutors should be ready to manifest their consciences to him, in confession, or secret, or in another manner, for the sake of the great profit this practice contains. Thus too they should be ready to make a general confession, from the last one they made, to the one whom the superior thinks it wise to designate in his place.

CHAPTER 2.   *What pertains to poverty and its consequences*

[553] 1.   Poverty, as the strong wall of the religious life, should be loved and preserved in its integrity as far as this is possible with God's grace. The enemy of the human race generally tries to weaken this defense and rampart which God our Lord inspired religious institutes to raise against him and the other adversaries of their perfection. Into what was well ordered by their first founders he induces alterations by means of interpretations and innovations not in conformity with those founders' spirit. Therefore, that provision may be made in this matter as far as lies in our power, all those who make profession in this Society should promise not to take part in altering what pertains to poverty in the Constitutions, unless it be in some manner to make it more strict, according to the circumstances in the Lord.

[555] 2.   In the houses or churches which the Society accepts to aid souls, it should not be licit to have any fixed revenue, even for the sacristy or building or anything else, in such a manner that any administration of this revenue is in the control of the Society. But the Society, relying on God our Lord whom it serves with the aid of His divine grace, should trust that without its having fixed revenue He will cause everything to

be provided which can be expedient for His greater praise and glory.

[561] 5. Not only fixed revenue, but also stable goods of any kind, should not be possessed by the houses or churches of the Society, either in particular or in common, except for what is necessary or highly expedient for the members' habitation and use. An example of this latter case would arise if some place apart from the common habitation should be accepted for those who are convalescing and those who withdraw there to devote themselves to spiritual matters, because of the better air or other advantages which it has. In such a case it should be something which is not rented to others and does not bring profits equivalent to fixed revenue.

[565] 7. All who are under the obedience of the Society should remember that they ought to give gratuitously what they have gratuitously received, without demanding or accepting any stipend or alms in recompense for Masses or confessions or preaching or lecturing or visiting or any other ministry among those which the Society may exercise according to our Institute, that thus it may proceed in the divine service with greater liberty and greater edification of the neighbor.

[569] 10. The members should be ready to beg from door to door when obedience or necessity requires it.

[570] 11. Just as no personal possession may be held in the house, so neither may one be held outside the house in the hands of another. Each one should be content with what is given to him from the common supply for his necessary or proper use, without any superfluity.

[572] 12. That poverty may be the better preserved in all its integrity. and also the tranquility which it brings with it, the individual professed or formed coadjutors will be incapable of receiving an inheritance; and more than this, not even the houses or churches or colleges will be able to do so through those individual members. In this way all lawsuits and contro-

versies will be more effectively eliminated and charity with all will be preserved to the glory of God our Lord.

[580] 16.   What pertains to food, sleep, and the use of the other things necessary or proper for living, will be ordinary and not different from that which appears good to the physician of the region where one lives, in such a manner that what each one subtracts from this will be withdrawn through his own devotion and not through obligation. Nevertheless there should be concern for the humility, poverty, and spiritual edification which we ought to keep always in view in our Lord.

CHAPTER 3.   The occupations which those in the Society should undertake and those which they should avoid

[582] 1.   In view of the time and approval of their life through which those wait before being admitted among the professed and even among the formed coadjutors, it is presupposed that they will be men who are spiritual and sufficiently advanced to run in the path of Christ our Lord to the extent that their bodily strength and the exterior occupations undertaken through charity and obedience allow. Therefore, in what pertains to prayer, meditation, and study and also in regard to the bodily practices of fasts, vigils, and other austerities or penances, it does not seem expedient to give them any other rule than that which discreet charity dictates to them [A], provided that the confessor should always be informed and also, when a doubt about expediency arises, the superior. The following statement is the only one which will be made in general. On the one hand, the members should keep themselves alert that the excessive use of these practices may not weaken the bodily energies and consume time to such an extent that these energies are insufficient for the spiritual help of one's fellowmen according to our Institute; and on the other hand, they should be vigilant that these practices may not be

relaxed to such an extent that the spirit grows cold and the human and lower passions grow warm.

[583] A.   If the superior thinks it expedient to give some subjects a determined time to keep them from being either excessive or deficient in their spiritual exercises, he will have the authority to do this. So too in regard to the use of the other means, if he judges in some case that one of these means ought to be employed without leaving this matter to the discretion of the individual, he will proceed in accordance with what God our Lord leads him to think proper. And the part of the subject will be to accept with complete devotion the order which is given to him.

[585] 3.   In regard to the particular rules which are employed in the houses where they happen to be, it is proper that they should endeavor to observe the part which is expedient either for their own progress and edification or for that of the rest among whom they find themselves, and which is proposed to them according to the judgment of the superior.

[586] 4.   Because the occupations which are undertaken for the aid of souls are of great importance, proper to our Institute, and very frequent; and because, on the other hand, our residence in one place or another is so highly uncertain, our members will not regularly hold choir for the canonical hours or sing Masses and offices. For one who experiences devotion in listening to those chanted services will suffer no lack of places where he can find his satisfaction; and it is expedient that our members should apply their efforts to the pursuits that are more proper to our vocation, for glory to God our Lord.

CHAPTER 4.   *The help given to the dying members and the suffrages after death*

[595] 1.   Both during his whole life and also and even more at the time of death, each member of the Society ought to strive

earnestly that through him God our Lord may be glorified and served and his fellowmen may be edified, at least by the example of his patience and fortitude along with his living faith, hope, and love of the eternal goods which Christ our Lord merited and acquired for us by those altogether incomparable sufferings of His temporal life and death. But sickness is often such that it greatly impairs the use of the mental faculties; and through the vehement attacks of the devil and the great importance of not succumbing to him, the passing away is itself such that the sick man needs help from fraternal charity. Therefore with great vigilance the superior should see to it that the one who in the physician's opinion is in danger should, before being deprived of his judgment, receive all the holy sacraments and fortify himself for the passage from this temporal life to that which is eternal, by means of the arms which the divine liberality of Christ our Lord offers.

[596] 2. He ought likewise to be aided by the very special prayers of all the residents of the house, until he has given up his soul to his Creator. Besides others who may enter to see the sick man die, in greater or less numbers according to the superior's judgment, some ought to be especially assigned to keep him company. They should encourage him and recall to his mind the helpful thoughts which are appropriate at that moment. When in time he can no longer be helped, they should commend him to God our Lord, until his soul now freed from the body is received by Him who redeemed it by that price so high, His blood and life.

CHAPTER 5.   *The Constitutions do not oblige under pain of sin*

[602] 1. The Society desires that all the Constitutions and Declarations and its regime of living should be observed in every regard according to our Institute, without deviation in anything; and on the other hand it also desires that its individual members may be free from anxiety or aided against falling

into any snare of sin which could arise through the obligation of these Constitutions or ordinations. For that reason our considered opinion in our Lord is that, apart from the express vow which the Society has with respect to the currently reigning sovereign pontiff, and apart from the other three essential vows of poverty, chastity, and obedience, no constitutions, declarations, or regime of living can oblige under mortal or venial sin, unless the superior orders the subjects in the name of our Lord Jesus Christ or in virtue of obedience, which may be done in regard to things and persons where it is judged to be highly expedient for the particular good of each one or for the universal good. Thus in place of the fear of giving offense there should arise a love and desire of all perfection, and a desire that greater glory and praise of Christ our Creator and Lord may follow.

PART VII. THE DISTRIBUTION OF THE INCORPORATED MEMBERS IN CHRIST'S VINEYARD AND THEIR RELA-. TIONS THERE WITH THEIR FELLOWMEN

CHAPTER 1. *Missions from the Holy Father*

[603] 1. Part VII deals with the members' duties toward their fellowmen (which is an end eminently characteristic of our Institute) when these members are dispersed to any part of Christ's vineyard, to labor in that part of it and in that work which have been entrusted to them. They may be sent to some places or others by the supreme vicar of Christ our Lord, or by the superiors of the Society, who for them are similarly in the place of His Divine Majesty; or they themselves may choose where and in what work they will labor, when they have been commissioned to travel to any place where they judge that greater service of God and the good of souls will follow; or they may carry on their labor, not by traveling but by residing

steadily and continually in certain places where much fruit of glory and service to God is expected.

Since one's being sent on a mission of His Holiness will be treated first, as being most important, it should be observed that the vow which the Society made to obey him as the supreme vicar of Christ without any excuse, meant that the members were to go to any place whatsoever where he judges it expedient to send them for the greater glory of God and the good of souls, whether among the faithful or the infidels [B]. The Society did not mean any particular place, but rather that it was to be distributed into diverse regions and places throughout the world, and it desired to proceed more correctly in this matter by leaving the distribution of its members to the sovereign pontiff.

[605] B. The intention of the fourth vow pertaining to the pope was not to designate a particular place but to have the members distributed throughout the various parts of the world. For those who first united to form the Society were from different provinces and realms and did not know into which regions they were to go, whether among the faithful or the unbelievers; and therefore, to avoid erring in the path of the Lord, they made that promise or vow in order that His Holiness might distribute them for greater glory to God. They did this in conformity with their intention to travel throughout the world and, when they could not find the desired spiritual fruit in one region, to pass on to another and another, ever intent on seeking the greater glory of God our Lord and the greater aid of souls.

[606] 2. In this matter, the Society has placed its own judgment and desire under that of Christ our Lord and His vicar; and neither the superior for himself nor any individual member of the Society will be able for himself or for another to arrange or to try to arrange, directly or indirectly, with the pope or his ministers to reside in or to be sent rather to one place than another. The individual members will leave this entire concern

to the supreme vicar of Christ and to their own superior; and in regard to his own person the superior will in our Lord leave this concern to His Holiness and to the Society.

[609] 3. Moreover, he who has been designated by His Holiness to go to some region should offer his person generously, without requesting provisions for the journey or causing a request for anything temporal to be made, except that His Holiness should order the member to be sent in the manner that His Holiness judges to be a greater service of God and of the Apostolic See, without taking thought about anything else.

[616] 7. When the residence in determined places must be prolonged and when it is possible without prejudice to the principal mission and intention of the sovereign pontiff, it will not be improper for the one on the mission to make some excursions to aid the souls in the neighboring regions and afterwards to return to his residence, if such excursions are possible and it appears to him that they could be fruitful in service to God our Lord. Likewise in the territory where he resides, he ought to attend with special care to the charge which was especially given to him and not to neglect it for other opportunities in the divine service, even good ones. Yet in addition to that charge he can and he ought to consider, but without prejudice to his mission, as has been said, in what other things he can employ himself for the glory of God and the good of souls. Thus he does not lose the opportunity for this which God sends him, to the extent that he will judge expedient in the Lord.

CHAPTER 2. *The missions received from the superior of the Society*

[618] 1. To be able to meet the spiritual needs of souls in many regions with greater facility and with greater security for those who go among them for this purpose [A], the superiors of the Society, according to the faculty granted by the sover-

eign pontiff,[3] will have authority to send any of the Society's members whomsoever [B] to whatsoever place these superiors think it more expedient to send them [C], although these members, wherever they are, will always be at the disposition of His Holiness.

However, there are many who request help while considering more their own spiritual obligations to their flocks, or other advantages not so immediately their own, rather than the common or universal benefits. Therefore the superior general, or whoever holds this authority from him, ought to bestow much careful thought on missions of this kind in order that, when he sends subjects to one region rather than to another [D], or for one purpose rather than for another [E], or one particular person rather than another or several of them [F], in this manner or in that [G], for a greater or lesser time [H], that procedure may always be used which is conducive to the greater service of God and the universal good.

If the superior thinks, while holding fast to this thoroughly right and pure intention in the presence of God our Lord, that it is wise because of the difficulty or importance of the decision, he will commend the matter to His Divine Majesty and cause it to be commended in the prayers and Masses of the house. He will also discuss it with one or more members of the Society who happen to be present and whom he thinks suitable. Then he himself will decide about sending or not sending, and about the other circumstances, as he will judge to be expedient for greater glory to God.

---

[3] The faculty to send the companions *"among the Christian faithful"* was given to the superior general by Paul III, "vivae vocis oraculo," some years after 1539 (MI *Const* I 162), probably not before 16 January 1543 (letter of Ignatius to Juan Bernardo Díaz de Luco, in which it appears that Ignatius does not yet have the faculty of sending subjects to Spain), certainly before 1544-45 (latest date of the document *Constitutiones de missionibus*); nevertheless the faculty of sending among the infidels was conceded by Paul III only in the bull *Licet debitum* of 18 October 1549 (MI *Const* I 358 [2]).

The part of him who is sent will be, without interposing himself in favor of going or remaining in one place rather than another, to leave the disposition of himself completely and freely to the superior who in the place of Christ our Lord directs him in the path of His greater service and praise [I]. In similar manner, too, no one ought to try by any means to bring it about that others will remain in one place or go to another, unless he does so with the approval of his superior, by whom he should be governed in our Lord [K].

[619] A. The superior of the Society can more easily and more expeditiously make provision for many places (especially those remote from the Apostolic See), than would be the case if those who need members of the Society must always approach the sovereign pontiff. For the individual members, too, there is greater security if they go from obedience to their superiors rather than through their own decision (even if they were capable of making it), and not as men sent by him whom they have in place of Christ to direct them as the interpreter of His divine will.

[620] B. Just as the general can perform the other functions by himself and through persons under him, so too can he perform this one of sending his subjects on missions, by reserving to himself the missions which he thinks should be thus reserved.

[621] C. The sending of subjects "to whatsoever place these superiors think it expedient" means either among the faithful, even though it be in the Indies, or among the unbelievers, especially where there is a colony of believers, as in Greece and elsewhere. Where the inhabitants are more exclusively unbelievers, the superior should ponder seriously in the sight of God our Lord whether he ought to send subjects or not, and where, and whom. The part of the subject will always be to accept his appointment joyfully as something from God our Lord.

[622] D. [a] To proceed more successfully in this sending of subjects to one place or another, one should keep the greater service of God and the more universal good before his eyes as the norm to hold oneself on the right course. It appears that in the vineyard of the Lord, which is so extensive, the following procedure of selection ought to be used. When other considerations are equal (and this should be understood in everything that follows), that part of the vineyard ought to be chosen which has greater need, because of the lack of other workers or because of the misery and weakness of one's fellowmen in it and the danger of their eternal condemnation.

[b] Consideration should also be given to where the greater fruit will probably be reaped through the means which the Society uses. This case would arise, for example, where one sees the door more widely open and a better disposition among the people along with compliancy favorable to their progress. This disposition consists in the people's greater devotion and desire (which can be judged in part by the insistence they show), or in the condition and quality of the persons who are more capable of making progress and of preserving the fruit produced, to the glory of God our Savior.

[c] In places where our indebtedness is greater, for example, where there is a house or college of the Society or where there are members of it who study and are the recipients of charitable deeds from those people, and when it is granted that the other considerations pertaining to spiritual progress are equal, it would be more fitting to have some laborers there, and for that reason to prefer these places to others, in conformity with perfect charity.

[d] The more universal the good is, the more is it divine. Therefore preference ought to be given to those persons and places which, through their own improvement, become a cause which can spread the good accomplished to many others who are under their influence or take guidance from them.

[e] For that reason, the spiritual aid which is given to important and public persons ought to be regarded as more important, since it is a more universal good. This is true whether these persons are laymen such as princes, lords, magistrates, or ministers of justice, or whether they are clerics such as prelates. The same also holds true of the spiritual aid which is given to persons distinguished for learning and authority, because of that reason of its being the more universal good. For that same reason, too, preference ought to be shown to the aid which is given to great nations such as the Indies, or to important cities, or to universities, which are generally attended by numerous persons who by being aided themselves can become laborers for the help of others.

[f] Similarly, the Society ought to labor more intensely in those places where the enemy of Christ our Lord has sown cockle, and especially where he has spread bad opinion about the Society or stirred up ill will against it so as to impede the fruit which the Society could produce. This is especially to be observed if the place is an important one of which account should be taken, by sending there, if possible, persons such that by their life and learning they may undo the evil opinion founded on false reports.

[623] E. [a] For better success in the choice of undertakings for which the superior sends his subjects, the same norm should be kept in view, namely, that of considering the greater divine honor and the greater universal good. This consideration can supply completely just reasons for sending a subject to one place rather than to another.

[b] To touch upon some motives which can exist in favor of one place or another, we mention these. First of all, the members of the Society may occupy themselves in undertakings directed toward benefits for the soul, and also in those directed toward benefits for the body through the practice of mercy and charity. Similarly, they may help some persons in matters pertaining to their greater perfection, or to their lesser perfec-

tion; and finally, in regard to things which are of themselves of more good, or of less good. In all these cases, if both things cannot be done simultaneously and the other considerations are equal, the spiritual goods ought to be preferred to the bodily, the matters of greater perfection to those of less, and the things more good to those less good.

[c] Likewise, when there are some things in the service of God our Lord which are more urgent, and others which are less pressing and can better suffer postponement of the remedy, even though they are of equal importance, the first ought to be preferred to the second.

[d] Similarly too, when there are some things which are especially incumbent upon the Society or it is seen that there are no others to attend to them, and other things in regard to which others do have care and a method of providing for them, in choosing missions there is reason to prefer the first to the second.

[e] Likewise also, among the pious works of equal importance, urgency, and need, when some are safer for the one who cares for them and others are more dangerous; and when some are easier and more quickly dispatched and others are more difficult and finished only in a longer time, the first should be similarly preferred over the second.

[f] When everything mentioned above is equal and when there are some occupations which are of more universal good and extend to the aid of more of our fellowmen, such as preaching or lecturing, and others which are concerned more with individuals, such as hearing confessions or giving Exercises; and when further it is impossible to accomplish both sets of occupations simultaneously, preference should be given to the first set, unless there should be some circumstances through which it would be judged that to take up the second set would be more expedient.

[g] Similarly too, when there are some spiritual works which

continue longer and are of more lasting value, such as certain pious foundations for the aid of our fellowmen, and other works less durable which give help on a few occasions and only for a short while, then it is certain that the first ought to be preferred to the second. Hence it is also certain that the superior of the Society ought to employ his subjects more in the first type rather than in the second, since that is a greater service to God and a greater good for our fellowmen.

[624] F. [a] Although it is the supreme providence and direction of the Holy Spirit that must efficaciously guide us to bring deliberations to a right conclusion in everything, and in sending to each place those who are more suitable and who will fit in better with the men and work to which they are sent, still this can be said in general. First, that for a matter of greater importance and one in which more depends on avoidance of error, as far as this depends on the part of the one who with God's grace must provide, subjects ought to be sent who are more select and in whom greater confidence is had.

[b] In matters which involve greater bodily labors, persons more strong and healthy.

[c] In matters which contain greater spiritual dangers, persons more approved in virtue and more reliable.

[d] To go to discreet persons who hold posts of spiritual or temporal government, those members seem most suitable who excel in discretion and grace of conversation and (while not lacking interior qualities) have a pleasing appearance which increases their prestige. For their counsel can be highly important.

[e] To treat with cultivated persons of talent and learning, those are more suitable who likewise have a special gift of skill and learning. For these persons can be more successful in lectures and conversations.

[f] For the ordinary people, those will generally be most apt who have talent for preaching, hearing confessions, and the

like.

[g] The number and combination of such laborers who are to be sent should also receive consideration. First of all, it would be wise when possible that one member should not be sent alone. At least two should be sent, that thus they may be more helpful to one another in spiritual and bodily matters and also, by distributing among themselves the labors in the service of their neighbor, be more profitable to those to whom they are sent.

[h] And if two set out, it seems that with a preacher or lecturer there could well go another who in confessions and spiritual exercises could gather in the harvest which the speaker prepares for him, and who could aid the speaker by conversations and the other means used in dealing with our fellowmen.

[i] Likewise, when one less experienced in the Society's manner of proceeding and of dealing with the neighbor is sent, it seems that he ought to be accompanied by another who has more experience in that procedure, whom he can imitate, with whom he can confer, and from whom he can take counsel in the perplexing matters which he encounters.

[j] With one very ardent and daring it seems that there could well go another more circumspect and cautious. Procedure similar to this, too, could be used in regard to other combinations, in such wise that the diversity may, when united by the bond of charity, be helpful to both of them and may not engender contradiction or discord, either among them or with their fellowmen.

[k] To send more than two when the importance of the work intended in the service of God our Lord is greater and requires a larger number, and when the Society can provide more laborers without prejudice to other things conducive to greater divine glory and universal good, is something which the superior will have authority to do, according as the unction of

the Holy Spirit inspires him or as he judges in the sight of His Divine Majesty to be better and more expedient.

[625] G. In regard to the manner in which he is to send them (after the proper instruction), the superior should deliberate whether he will send them in the manner of the poor, so that they would go on foot and without money, or with better facilities; whether with letters to be helpful toward winning acceptance and benevolence at their destination; and whether these letters should be addressed to individuals, or the city, or its head. In regard to all the details, the superior will consider the greater edification of the neighbor and the service of God our Lord and then decide what should be done.

[626] H. When no limitation has been set by the sovereign pontiff as regards the time for which some laborers are sent to one place and others to another, it seems that the length of their stay ought to be regulated by the following considerations. Thought should be given to the nature of the spiritual affairs being dealt with, to the greater or less importance the men themselves have as viewed against the need and the fruit which is being reaped or expected. Then, too, attention must be given to the opportunities available in other places, to the obligation there is to take up these works, and to the resources which the Society possesses to provide for these other undertakings. One should also weigh the accidents which can intervene to shorten or prolong the time. Finally, one should attend to the first characteristic of our Institute. Since this is to travel through some regions and others, remaining for a shorter or longer time in proportion to the fruit which is seen, it will be necessary to judge whether it is expedient to give more time or less to certain missions or to others. That this may be perceived, it is important that those who are sent should keep the superior informed by frequent reports about the fruit which is reaped. When it is necessary to change someone, the superior should remember that in recalling him he should, as far as possible, use such means that those from among whom he is

taken will retain all their benevolence rather than suffer a certain disedification, being persuaded that in everything the honor and glory of God and the universal good are being sought.

[627] I. For someone to propose the motions or thoughts which occur to him contrary to an order received, meanwhile submitting his entire judgment and will to the judgment and will of his superior who is in the place of Christ, is not against this prescription.

[628] K. By this it is clearly forbidden that any member should influence some prince, or community, or person of authority to write a request to the superior for some member of the Society or to ask this of him by word of mouth, unless the member has first communicated the matter to the superior and understood this procedure to be his will.

CHAPTER 3. A member's free movement from one place to another

[633] 1. It is the part of those who live under obedience to the Society not to scheme, directly or indirectly, to be sent here or there, either by His Holiness or by their own superior in the name of Christ our Lord. Nevertheless one who is sent to an extensive region such as the Indies or other provinces and for whom no particular district is marked out, may remain in one place for a longer or shorter period. Or, after considering the reasons on one side and the other, while praying and keeping his will indifferent, he may travel about wherever he judges this to be more expedient for the glory of God our Lord.

From this it is clear that, without swerving from that foremost and supreme order of His Holiness, in missions of this type the superior will have much greater power to direct a member to one place rather than another, as he judges in the Lord to be expedient.

[634] 2. Wherever anyone is stationed, if he is not limited to the use of some means such as lecturing or preaching, he may use the means which he judges more suitable among those which the Society employs. They have been mentioned in Part IV and will be mentioned again in the following chapter. Similarly, he will avoid what those passages disapprove, for greater service to God.

CHAPTER 4. Ways in which the houses and colleges can help their fellowmen

[636] 1. Since the Society endeavors to aid its fellowmen not merely by traveling through diverse regions but also by residing continually in some places, for example, in the houses and colleges, it is important to have learned the ways in which souls can be helped in those places, in order to use that selection of these ways which is possible for the glory of God our Lord.

[637] 2. The first way that comes to mind is the good example of a thoroughly upright life and of Christian virtue, through the effort to edify by good deeds no less but rather more than by words those with whom one deals.

[638] 3. Likewise, the neighbor is aided by desires in the presence of God our Lord and by prayers for all the Church, especially for those persons in it who are of greater importance for the common good [A]. They should also pray for friends and benefactors, living and dead, whether they request these prayers or not. Similarly, let them pray for those for whose special benefit they and the other members of the Society are working in diverse places among believers or unbelievers, that God may dispose them all to receive His grace through the feeble instruments of this least Society.

[639] A. Examples of such persons are the ecclesiastical princes, the secular princes, and other persons who have great

power to promote or impede the good of souls and the divine service.

[640] 4. Furthermore, aid can be given by Masses and other divine services which, whether they are said at the request of individuals or merely for the devotion of the celebrant, are to be celebrated without accepting any alms. In regard to the Masses, beyond those said for the founders, one or two or more Masses (according to the number of priests and their convenience) should be ordered each week for the benefactors living and dead. Thus God is begged to accept this Holy Sacrifice for them and through His infinite and sovereign liberality to requite with eternal recompense that liberality which they have shown to the Society because of their love and reverence for Him.

[642] 5. Further still, the neighbor can be aided through the administration of the sacraments, especially the hearing of confessions (with some priests being assigned by the superior for this service), and through administering Holy Communion, apart from the Communion of Easter time received in the communicant's parish church.

[645] 6. In the church the word of God should be proposed to the people unremittingly by means of sermons, lectures, and the teaching of Christian doctrine, by those whom the superior approves and designates for this work, and at the times and in the manner which he judges to be most conducive to greater divine glory and edification of souls.

[648] 8. Likewise, they will endeavor to be profitable to individuals by spiritual conversations, by counseling and exhorting to good works, and by conducting Spiritual Exercises [F].

[649] F. The Spiritual Exercises should not be given in their entirety except to a few persons, namely, those of such a character that from their progress notable fruit is expected for the glory of God. But the exercises of the first week can be

made available to large numbers; and some examinations of conscience and methods of prayer (especially the first of those which are touched on in the Exercises) can also be given far more widely; for anyone who has good will seems to be capable of these exercises.

[650] 9. The members will also occupy themselves in corporal works of mercy to the extent that the more important spiritual activities permit and their own energies allow. For example, they can help the sick, especially those in hospitals, by visiting them and by sending others to serve them. They can reconcile the disaffected and do what they can for the poor and for prisoners in the jails, both by their personal work and by getting others to do it. How much of all this is expedient to do will be regulated by the discretion of the superior, who will keep always in view the greater service of God and the universal good.

[653] 11. One who has talent to write books useful for the common good ought to do so.

PART VIII. HELPS TOWARD UNITING THE DISTANT MEMBERS WITH THEIR HEAD AND AMONG THEMSELVES

CHAPTER 1. *Aids toward the union of hearts*

[655] 1. The more difficult it is for the members of this congregation to be united with their head and among themselves, since they are so scattered among the faithful and among the unbelievers in diverse regions of the world [A], the more ought means to be sought for that union. For the Society cannot be preserved, or governed, or, consequently, attain the end it seeks for the greater glory of God unless its members are united among themselves and with their head. Therefore the present treatise will deal first with what can aid the union of hearts and later with helps toward the union of persons in

congregations or chapters.[4] With respect to the union of hearts, some of the helpful means lie on the side of the subjects, others on the side of the superiors, and others on both sides.[5]

[656] A. There are also other reasons, for example, the fact that ordinarily they will be learned men, that they will have the favor of princes or important persons, or of peoples, and so forth.

[657] 2. On the side of the subjects, it will be helpful neither to admit a large crowd of persons to profession nor to retain any other than select persons even as formed coadjutors or scholastics [B]. For a large number of persons whose vices are not well mortified is an obstruction to order and that union which is in Christ our Lord so necessary for the preservation of this Society's good condition and manner of proceeding.

[658] B. This does not exclude the number, even though it is very large, of persons who are suitable for profession or for the formed coadjutors or the approved scholastics. But it recommends avoidance of leniency in regarding as fit those who are not, especially for admission among the professed. When that

---

[4] This last sentence indicates first of all the structure of Part VIII: union of hearts (Chapter 1), union of the members of the Congregations (Chapters 2-4). The correlation between the sections reflects the correspondence between the *soul* (= heart, understood in the biblical sense, the interiority of man in his religious dimension in relation with God) and the *person* (= the person considered in his visible and external dimension). In this way, from the union of hearts (= union in its deepest interior dimension) we pass on to treat of the visible and external union, which manifests itself and is realized in the General Congregations.

[5] This last paragraph explains the structure of Chapter 1: what serves to help on the side of the subjects (*Const* [656-665]); what serves to help on the side of the superiors (*Const* [666-670]); what serves to help on both sides (*Const* [671-676]). To understand the importance of this chapter, it is good to remember that the union of hearts and minds was the first reality affirmed by the early Fathers in the deliberations of the spring of 1539, which, as is well known, resulted in the foundation of the Society of Jesus (*MI Const* I 3 [3]).

which was stated in Part I and Part V is well observed, enough will be done. For a group of members of that quality, even if it is numerous, is not to be regarded as a crowd, but as an elite race.

[659] 3.   Since this union is produced in great part by the bond of obedience, this virtue should always be maintained in its vigor; and those who are sent out from the houses to labor in the Lord's field should as far as possible be persons practiced in this virtue. Those who are more important in the Society should give a good example of obedience to the others, by being closely united to their own superior and by obeying him promptly, humbly, and devoutly. Thus too one who has not given a good example of this virtue ought at least to go in the company of someone who has given it; because in general a companion more advanced in obedience will help one who is less so, with the divine favor.

[662] 4.   To this same virtue of obedience is related the properly observed subordination of the superiors, one to another, and of the subjects to the superiors, in such wise that the individuals dwelling in some house or college have recourse to their local superior or rector and are governed by him in every respect. Those who are distributed throughout the province refer to the provincial or some other local superior who is closer, according to the orders they received; and all the local superiors or rectors should communicate often with the provincial and thus too be directed by him in everything; and the provincials in their turn will deal in the same way with the general. For this subordination, when well observed in this manner, will preserve the union which is attained chiefly through it, with the help of the grace of God our Lord.

[664] 5.   One who is seen to be a cause of division among those who live together, estranging them either among themselves or from their head, ought with great diligence to be separated from that community, as a pestilence which can infect it seriously if a remedy is not quickly applied [F].

[665] F. To separate can mean either to expel the person from the Society completely or to transfer him to another place, if this seems sufficient and more expedient for the divine service and the common good, in the judgment of him who has charge of the matter.

[666] 6. On the side of the superior general, that which will aid toward this union of hearts consists in the qualities of his person [G]. They will be treated in Part IX. With them he will carry on his office, which is to be for all the members a head from whom descends to all of them the impulse necessary for the end which the Society seeks. Thus it is that from the general as the head flows all the authority of the provincials, and from the provincials that of the local superiors, and from that of these local superiors that of the individual members. Thus too from that same head come the assignments to missions; or at least they come by his mandate and approval.

[667] G. Among other qualities, his good reputation and prestige among his subjects will be very specially helpful; and so will his having and manifesting love and concern for them, in such a way that the subjects hold the opinion that their superior has the knowledge, desire, and ability to rule them well in our Lord. For this and many other matters he will find it profitable to have with him persons able to give good counsel, as will be stated in Part IX, whose help he can use in what he must order for the Society's good manner of proceeding in diverse regions, unto divine glory.

Further help will be found in his having his method of commanding well thought out and organized, through his endeavoring to maintain obedience in the subjects in such a manner that the superior on his part uses all the love and modesty and charity possible in our Lord, so that the subjects can dispose themselves to have always toward their superiors greater love than fear, even though both are useful at times. He can also do this by referring some matters to them when it appears probable that they will be helped by this; and at other times, by going along with them to some extent and sympathizing with them when this, it seems, could be more expedient.

[671] 8. The chief bond to cement the union of the members among themselves and with their head is, on both sides, the love of God our Lord. For when the superior and the subjects are closely united to His Divine and Supreme Goodness, they will very easily be united among themselves, through that same love which will descend from the Divine Goodness and spread to all other men, and particularly into the body of the Society. Thus from both sides charity will come to further this union between superiors and subjects, and in general all goodness and virtues through which one proceeds in conformity with the spirit. Consequently there will also come total contempt of temporal things, in regard to which self-love, the chief enemy of this union and universal good, frequently induces disorder.

Still another great help can be found in uniformity, both interior uniformity of doctrine, judgments, and wills, as far as this is possible, and exterior uniformity in respect to clothing, ceremonies of the Mass, and other such matters, to the extent that the different qualities of persons, places, and the like, permit.

[673] 9. Still another very special help will be found in the exchange of letters between the subjects and the superiors, through which they learn about one another frequently and hear the news and reports which come from the various regions. The superiors, especially the general and the provincials, will take charge of this, by providing an arrangement through which each region can learn from the others whatever promotes mutual consolation and edification in our Lord.

PART IX. THE SOCIETY'S HEAD AND THE GOVERNMENT DESCENDING FROM HIM

CHAPTER 1. The need of a superior general and his lifelong term of office

[719] In all well-organized communities or congregations there must be, besides the persons who take care of the particular goals, one or several whose proper duty is to attend to the universal good. So too in this Society, in addition to those who have charge of its single houses or colleges and of its single provinces where it has those houses or colleges, there must be someone who holds that charge of the entire body of the Society, one whose duty is the good government, preservation, and development of the whole body of the Society; and this person is the superior general. There is a possibility of electing him in either of two ways, namely, for a determined period or for his whole life. But since his experience and practice of government, his knowledge of the individual members, and the prestige he has with them are a great aid in performing this office well, his election will be for life and not for a determined period. Thus too the Society, being universally occupied with important matters in the divine service, will be less disturbed and distracted by general congregations.

CHAPTER 2. The kind of person the superior general should be

[723] 1. In regard to the qualities which are desirable in the superior general, the first is that he should be closely united with God our Lord and intimate with Him in prayer and all his actions, that from God, the fountain of all good, the general may so much the better obtain for the whole body of the Society a large share of His gifts and graces, and also great power and efficacy for all the means which will be used for the help of souls.

[725] 2. The second quality is that he should be a person whose example in the practice of all virtues is a help to the other members of the Society. Charity should be especially resplendent in him, toward all his fellowmen and above all toward the members of the Society; and genuine humility too should shine forth, that these characteristics may make him highly lovable to God our Lord and to men.

[726] 3. He ought also to be independent of all passions, by his keeping them controlled and mortified, so that in his interior they may not disturb the judgment of his intellect and in his exterior he may be so composed, particularly so self-controlled when speaking, that no one, whether a member of the Society who should regard him as a mirror and model, or an extern, may observe in him any thing or word which does not edify him.

[727] 4. However, he should know how to mingle rectitude and necessary severity with kindness and gentleness to such an extent that he neither allows himself to swerve from what he judges to be more pleasing to God our Lord nor ceases to have proper sympathy for his sons. Thus although they are being reprimanded or punished, they will recognize that in what he does he is proceeding rightly in our Lord and with charity, even though it is against their liking according to the lower man.

[728] 5. Magnanimity and fortitude of soul are likewise highly necessary for him to bear the weaknesses of many, to initiate great undertakings in the service of God our Lord, and to persevere in them with constancy when it is called for, without losing courage in the face of the contradictions (even though they come from persons of high rank and power) and without allowing himself to be moved by their entreaties or threats from what reason and the divine service require. He should be superior to all eventualities, without letting himself be exalted by those which succeed or depressed by those which go poorly, being altogether ready to receive death, if necessary,

for the good of the Society in the service of Jesus Christ, God and our Lord.

[729] 6. The third quality is that he ought to be endowed with great understanding and judgment, in order that this talent may not fail him either in the speculative or the practical matters which may arise. And although learning is highly necessary for one who will have so many learned men in his charge, still more necessary is prudence along with experience in spiritual and interior matters, that he may be able to discern the various spirits and to give counsel and remedies to so many who will have spiritual necessities.

He also needs discretion in exterior matters and a manner of handling such diverse affairs as well as of conversing with such various persons from within and without the Society.

[730] 7. The fourth quality, one highly necessary for the execution of business, is that he should be vigilant and solicitous to undertake enterprises as well as energetic in carrying them through to their completion and perfection, rather than careless and remiss in such a way that he leaves them begun and not finished.

[731] 8. The fifth quality has reference to the body. In regard to health, appearance, and age, on the one hand account should be taken of propriety and prestige, and on the other hand of the physical energies which his charge requires, that in it he may be able to fulfill his office to the glory of God our Lord.

[733] 9. The sixth quality pertains to extrinsic endowments. Among these, preference ought to be given to those which help more toward edification and the service of God in such a charge. Examples are generally found in reputation, high esteem, and whatever else aids toward prestige with those within and without.

[735] 10. Finally, he ought to be one of those who are most outstanding in every virtue, most deserving in the Society, and

known as such for a considerable time. If any of the aforementioned qualities should be wanting, there should at least be no lack of great probity and of love for the Society, nor of good judgment accompanied by sound learning. For in regard to other things, the aids which he will have (and which will be treated below) could through God's help and favor supply to a great extent for many deficiencies.

CHAPTER 3. The superior general's authority over the society and his functions

[736] 1. It is judged altogether proper for the good government of the Society that the superior general should have complete authority over it, in order to build it up.

[746] 8. Just as it pertains to the general to see to it that the Constitutions of the Society are observed in all places, so too he will have power to grant dispensations in particular cases which require such dispensation, while he takes account of the persons, places, times, and other circumstances. He will use this power with the discretion which the Eternal Light gives him, meanwhile keeping his attention fixed on the purpose of the Constitutions, which is the greater divine service and the good of those who live in this Institute. He may use this power in what pertains to the experiences of those who are in probation, as also in other matters where such dispensation is judged to be the intention of those who enacted the Constitutions, for the glory of God our Lord.

[749] 9. The same general will also have complete authority over the missions, but in no case may he obstruct missions of the Apostolic See, as is stated in Part VII. From among those who are under his obedience he may send all, professed or not professed, to any regions of the world, for the time which seems good to him, whether it is definite or indefinite, in order to exercise any of the means which the Society uses to aid its fellowmen. Similarly, he may recall those sent, acting in

everything as he judges to be conducive to the greater glory of God.

[811] I. From what has been said about the general it will be possible to infer what is applicable to the provincial superiors, local superiors, and rectors of colleges, with respect to their qualities, authority, function, and the aids which each one ought to have. It will be possible to state all this expressly in the rules which pertain to each of these superiors.

PART X. HOW THE WHOLE BODY OF THE SOCIETY CAN BE PRESERVED AND DEVELOPED IN ITS WELL-BEING

[812] 1. The Society was not instituted by human means; neither is it through them that it can be preserved and developed, but through the omnipotent hand of Christ, God and our Lord. Therefore in Him alone must be placed the hope that He will preserve and carry forward what He deigned to begin for His service and praise and for the aid of souls. In conformity with this hope, the first and best proportioned means will be prayers and Masses which ought to be offered for this holy intention through their being ordered for it every week, month, and year in all the regions where the Society resides.

[813] 2. For the preservation and development not only of the body or exterior of the Society but also of its spirit, and for the attainment of the objective it seeks, which is to aid souls to reach their ultimate and supernatural end, the means which unite the human instrument with God and so dispose it that it may be wielded dexterously by His divine hand are more effective than those which equip it in relation to men. Such means are, for example, goodness and virtue, and especially charity, and a pure intention of the divine service, and familiarity with God our Lord in spiritual exercises of devotion, and sincere zeal for souls for the sake of glory to Him who created

and redeemed them and not for any other benefit. Thus it appears that care should be taken in general that all the members of the Society may devote themselves to the solid and perfect virtues and to spiritual pursuits, and attach greater importance to them than to learning and other natural and human gifts. For they are the interior gifts which make those exterior means effective toward the end which is sought.

[814] 3. When based upon this foundation, the natural means which equip the human instrument of God our Lord to deal with his fellowmen will all be helps toward the preservation and development of this whole body, provided they are acquired and exercised for the divine service alone; employed, indeed, not that we may put our confidence in them, but that we may cooperate with the divine grace according to the arrangement of the sovereign providence of God our Lord. For he desires to be glorified both through the natural means, which He gives as Creator, and through the supernatural means, which He gives as the Author of grace. Therefore the human or acquired means ought to be sought with diligence, especially well-grounded and solid learning, and a method of proposing it to the people by means of sermons, lectures, and the art of dealing and conversing with men.

[815] 4. In similar manner, great help will be derived from maintaining the colleges in their good state and discipline, by having the superintendence over them exercised by those who cannot receive any temporal gain, such as members of the professed Society, which will take care that those who possess the talent for it may receive formation in life and learning worthy of a Christian. For these students will be a seedbed for the professed Society and its coadjutors. Furthermore, if universities over which the Society exercises superintendence are added to the colleges, they too will aid toward the same end, as long as the method of procedure described in Part IV is preserved.

[816] 5. Since poverty is like a bulwark of religious institutes

which preserves them in their existence and discipline and defends them from many enemies; and since the devil uses corresponding effort to destroy this bulwark in one way or another, it will be highly important for the preservation and development of this whole body that every appearance of avarice should be banished afar, through the Society's abstention from accepting fixed income, or any possessions, or salaries for preaching, or lecturing, or Masses, or administration of sacraments, or spiritual things, as is stated in Part VI, and also through its avoidance of converting the fixed revenue of the colleges to its own utility.

[819] 7. Much aid is given toward perpetuating the well-being of this whole body by what was said in Part I, Part II, and Part V about avoiding the admission of a crowd, or of persons unsuitable for our Institute, even to probation, and about dismissals during the time of probation when it is found that some persons do not turn out to be suitable. Much less ought those to be retained who are addicted to vice or are incorrigible. But even greater strictness should be shown in admitting persons among the approved scholastics and formed coadjutors, and strictness far greater still in regard to admission to profession. The profession should be made only by persons who are selected for their spirit of learning, thoroughly and lengthily tested, and known with edification and satisfaction to all after various proofs of virtue and abnegation of themselves. This procedure is used that, even though the numbers are multiplied, the spirit may not be diminished or weakened, when those who are incorporated into the Society are such as have been described.

[820] 8. Since the well-being or illness of the head has its consequences in the whole body, it is supremely important that the election of the superior general be carried out as directed in Part IX. Next in importance is the choice of the lower superiors in the provinces, colleges, and houses of the Society. For in a general way, the subjects will be what these superiors

are.

It is also highly important that, in addition to that choice, the individual superiors should have much authority over the subjects, and the general over the individual superiors; and, on the other hand, that the Society have much authority over the general, as is explained in Part IX. This arrangement is made that all may have full power for good and that, if they do poorly, they may be kept under complete control.

It is similarly important that the superiors have suitable ministers, as was said in the same Part, for the organization and execution of the affairs pertaining to their office.

[821] 9. Whatever helps toward the union of the members of this Society among themselves and with their head will also help much toward preserving the well-being of the Society. This is especially the case with the bond of wills, which is the mutual charity and love they have for one another. This bond is strengthened by their getting information and news from one another and by having much intercommunication, by their following one same doctrine, and by their being uniform in everything as far as possible, and above all by the link of obedience, which unites the individuals with their superiors, and the local superiors among themselves and with the provincials, and both the local superiors and provincials with the general, in such a way that the subordination of some to others is diligently preserved.

[822] 10. Temperate restraint in spiritual and bodily labors and similar moderation in relation to the Constitutions, which do not lean toward an extreme of rigor or toward excessive laxity (and thus they can be better observed), will help this entire body to persevere in its good state and to be maintained in it.

[823] 11. Toward the same purpose it is helpful in general to strive to retain the good will and charity of all, even of those outside the Society, and especially of those whose favorable or

unfavorable attitude toward it is of great importance for opening or closing the gate leading to the service of God and the good of souls. It is also helpful that in the Society there should neither be nor be seen partiality to one side or another among Christian princes or rulers, but in its stead a universal love which embraces in our Lord all parties (even though they are adversaries to one another).

[826] 13.   It will also be helpful that attention should be devoted to the preservation of the health of the individual members, as was stated in Part III; and finally, that all should apply themselves to the observance of the Constitutions. For this purpose they must know them, at least those which pertain to each one. Therefore, each one should read or hear them every month.

PART TWO

ORIENTATIONS
FROM THE GENERAL CONGREGATIONS
AND THE FATHERS GENERAL

I. THE FUNDAMENTAL EXPERIENCE FROM WHICH FLOW THE MISSION AND LIFE OF A JESUIT

1. Sent by Christ

The Society has its origin in the Spiritual Exercises made by Saint Ignatius and his companions. They had heard the invitation of Christ the King and had followed it; for that reason they not only dedicated themselves entirely to labor, but desiring to become outstanding in every service of their King, they made offerings of greater worth and importance, so that they would be sent under the banner of Christ by Him into the entire world, spreading his teachings among all degrees and conditions of men. *(GC31 d. 1 n. 2)*

2. The mission under the Roman Pontiff

They offered and dedicated themselves and their lives to Christ our Lord and to His true and legitimate vicar on earth; so that he as Vicar of Christ might dispose of them and might send them where he judged they could bear greater fruit. Thus it came about that the promise made to God of obeying the Roman Pontiff with regard to all missions turned out to be "our beginning and first foundation." *(GC31 d. 1 nn. 3-4)*

Now, in a spirit of faith, our Society confirms again the traditional bond of love and service which united it with the Roman Pontiff. We wish to respond to his desires expressed on various occasions and to carry out his missions. At the same time we intend to cooperate with the College of Bishops in its service of the Gospel. *(GC33 d. 1 n. 7)*

3. *United in a single body*

The first mission entrusted to them by Paul III was one that was likely to scatter the group of Fathers in all directions. Therefore, after many deliberations in which they tried to distinguish between various spiritual inspirations and weigh the reasons for each side carefully, these first Fathers decided that they should not break up "a society united in God," but rather gradually strengthen it and stabilize it by making themselves into a unified body. Indeed they judged it more expedient to give their obedience to one of their number that they might more successfully and perfectly carry out their first desire of fulfilling the divine will in all things. Thus also the Society would be more securely preserved. *(GC31 d. 1, n. 3)*

4. *The Spiritual Exercises in our vocation*

To maintain faithfully the grace of our vocation as described in the Institute, the Spiritual Exercises of our holy founder stand in first place, both as a perennial source of those interior gifts upon which depends our effectiveness in reaching the goal set before us, and as the living expression of the Ignatian spirit which must temper and interpret all our laws. *(GC31 d. 4 n. 2)*

In the Spiritual Exercises we are able continually to renew our faith and apostolic hope by experiencing again the love of God in Christ Jesus. We strengthen our commitment to be companions of Jesus in His mission, to labor like Him in solidarity with the poor and with Him for the establishment of the Kingdom. *(GC32 d. 4 n. 38)*

The Society supposes that we are "men formed by the Exercises" and genuinely tested by this foremost of our experiences, men who are continually renewing themselves in the dispositions of the Exercises. Different vocations each have their own respective charisms. For us nothing can replace the experience of the Exercises for maintaining both one's personal equilibrium and the unity of the Society. *(Fr. Pedro Arrupe, AR XV 29)*

5. *To live in Christ, personal love for Christ*

What is it to be a Jesuit? It is to know that one is a sinner, yet called to be a companion of Jesus as Ignatius was: Ignatius, who begged the Blessed Virgin to "place him with her Son," and who then saw the Father himself ask Jesus, carrying his Cross, to take this pilgrim into his company. *(GC32 d. 2 n. 1)*

We seek to preach the Gospel in a personal love for the Person of Jesus Christ, asking daily for an ever more inward knowledge of Him, that we may better love Him and follow Him; Jesus, whom we seek, as St. Ignatius sought, to experience; Jesus, Son of God, sent to serve, sent to set free, put to death, and risen from the dead. This love is the deepest wellspring of our action and our life. *(GC32 d. 2 nn. 26-27)*

From this love for Christ, the Society offers itself completely to the Church, so that the Supreme Pontiff, as the Vicar of Christ, may "send" all its members into the vineyard of the Lord. *(GC31 d. 1 n. 6)*

6. *A life illumined by faith*

Faith, progressively encompassing all reality, must permeate us as persons if we are to give authentic witness to the living presence of Christ the Lord. *(GC31 d. 14 n. 3)*

The Jesuit will see, with a deep faith, God's active presence and his plan of salvation in the aspirations, conflicts, and miseries of the human race in its present stage of development. He will recognize natural and human values, foster them in himself and others, raise them to a higher plane by consecrating them in their entirety to God, and guard himself against falling a victim to naturalism or letting his faith become weak and lifeless. *(Fr. Pedro Arrupe, AR XV 109)*

Faithful to the inspiration of Ignatius, the first question which we ought to pose to ourselves is about our experience of God in our following of Christ, in their Spirit, which animates the life and activity of the Society of Jesus. That this is the primordial question is affirmed when the Formula of the Institute proclaims "let a man look first to God"; and even though the Formula must go on to consider the purpose of the Society, it does so in terms of a journey to God: "and then to the nature of the Institute which is, so to speak, a pathway to God." *(Fr. Peter-Hans Kolvenbach, AR XIX 1063-4)*

7. A way of life inseparably apostolic and religious

Since the goal to which the Society directly tends is "to help our own souls and the souls of our neighbor to attain the ultimate end for which they were created," it is necessary that our life—of priests as well as of scholastics and brothers—be undividedly apostolic and religious. This intimate connection between the religious and apostolic aspects in the Society ought to animate our whole way of living, praying, and working, and impress on it an apostolic character. *(GC31 d. 13 n. 3)*

The grace of Christ, which enables and impels us to seek "the salvation and perfection of souls"—or what might be called, in contemporary terms, the total and integral liberation of man, leading to participation in the life of God himself—is the same grace by which we are enabled and impelled to seek "our own salvation and perfection." *(GC32 d. 2 n. 11)*

8. The "magis," abnegation, and humility

Following St. Ignatius' terminology, "let us consider as addressed to ourselves" each of the great themes, long familiar yet ever inexhaustible; for example, the dynamic power of that "magis" which excludes any form of mediocrity; that interior abnegation which is a condition for making a choice of what is better; the call of our Lord inviting us to personal friendship with Him; God's will that we should love and serve Him in everyone and in everything, preferring those matters which advance us toward greater freedom from self-love. *(Fr. Pedro Arrupe, AR XV 29)*

We cannot attain this discerning attitude without self-abnegation. Sign of our joy at the approach of the Kingdom and result of a progressive identification with Christ who "emptied himself being born in the likeness of man," this abnegation is required by the Spiritual Exercises: to divest ourselves of "self-love, self-will, and self-interest." It is only through detachment from all we have and are, that we can receive all from God in faith and give ourselves wholly to others in love. Without such an attitude we cannot present ourselves as interiorly free enough for the authentic service of Him who calls us. *(GC33 d. 1 n. 13)*

We preserve the ambition to preach the Gospel "in humility": but we realize that there are many enterprises of great worth and moment in the Church and in the world which we, as priests and religious inspired by one particular charism, are not in a position to undertake. And even in those enterprises which we can and should undertake, we realize that we must be willing to work with others: with Christians, men of other religious faiths, and all men of good will; willing to play a subordinate, supporting, anonymous role; and willing to learn how to serve from those we seek to serve.

This availability for the meanest tasks, or at least the desire to be thus available, is part of the identity of the Jesuit. When he offers to distinguish himself in the service of the Eternal King, when he asks to be received under His standard, when he glories with Ignatius in being placed by the Father "with the Son," he does so not in any spirit of prideful privilege, but in the spirit of Him who "emptied Himself to assume the condition of a slave, even to accepting death, death on a cross." *(GC32 d. 2 nn. 29-30)*

Deeply conscious of our utter unworthiness for so great a mission, relying only on God's love and grace, we offer together the prayer of Ignatius: Take, O Lord, and receive all my liberty, my memory, my understanding, and my entire will. Whatever I have or hold, You have given to me; I restore it all to You, and surrender it wholly to be governed by Your will. Give me only Your love and Your grace, and I am rich enough and ask for nothing more. *(GC32 d. 2 n. 32)*

II. OUR APOSTOLIC LIFE

A. Fundamental Features

9. *On a mission*

Our Society was founded principally for the defense and propagation of the faith and for the rendering of any service in the Church that may be for the glory of God and the common good.

At the very center of that insight is the sense of mission. No sooner was our Society born than it placed itself at the disposal of "the Roman Pontiff, Christ's Vicar on earth," to be sent wherever there is hope of God's greater glory and the service of men.

A Jesuit, therefore, is essentially a man on a mission: a mission which he receives immediately from the Holy Father and from his own religious superiors, but ultimately from

Christ himself, the one sent by the Father. It is by being sent that the Jesuit becomes a companion of Jesus. *(GC32 d. 2 nn. 11, 13-14)*

10. *In the Church*

Seeking to lead a life worthy of the vocation to which we have been called, the Society commits itself again to serving the Church in her teaching, life and worship, and helping her to offer to the world "all that she herself is, all that she believes." In the spirit of St. Ignatius, we wish to show our commitment "not less but rather more in good works than in words," for the edification of those with whom we work, so that we may become more generous servants of the people God has gathered for the world's salvation. *(GC33 d. 1 n. 6)*

Let the entire Society seek to incorporate itself more and more vigorously and creatively in the life of the Church so that we may experience and live its mystery within ourselves. Thus we may be indeed for the people of God servants of the joy of the Lord. *(GC33 d. 1 n. 8)*

Meditation on the Rules for Thinking with the Church suggests a positive, creative feeling. Called to praise God our Lord, in the words of the principle and foundation, man has been created to praise Him for all the life He calls forth in His Church, in whatever form and through the most diverse gifts. This positive attitude, founded on praise and thanksgiving for what God is accomplishing before our very eyes amongst his people, was learnt by Ignatius under the standard of Christ, who wants to preserve, construct and build up; the destructive power, leading to death, is written on the standard of Satan. *(Fr. Peter-Hans Kolvenbach, AR XIX 1087)*

The apostolic orientation of the Society must be inserted into the entire apostolate of the Church, of the people of God, and it must be carried out in complete and loyal collaboration with all the apostolic forces of the Church, of bishops and of priests, of religious families and of ecclesial movements, and of the laity.

Hence there is need to discern with great openness what could be the specific contribution of the Society, faithful to its charism in and for the Church, with the generous collaboration of the people of God. *(Fr. Peter-Hans Kolvenbach, AR XIX 1072)*

11. *In companionship*

It is in companionship that the Jesuit fulfills his mission. He belongs to a community of friends in the Lord who, like him, have asked to be received under the standard of Christ the King. This community is the entire body of the Society itself, no matter how widely dispersed over the face of the earth. The particular local community to which he may belong at any given moment is, for him, simply a concrete—if, here and now, privileged—expression of this world-wide brotherhood. *(GC32 d. 2 nn. 15-16)*

B. Conditions of Our Service

12. *Apostolic contemplation of the world*

St. Ignatius and his first companions, in the spiritual experience of the Exercises, were moved to a searching consideration of the world of their own time in order to discover its needs. They contemplated "how the Three Divine Persons look down upon the whole expanse or circuit of all the earth, filled with human beings" and decide "that the Second Person should become man to save the human race." Then they turned their eyes to where God's gaze was fixed, and saw for themselves the men and women of their time, one after another, "with such great diversity in dress and in manners of acting. Some are white, some black; some at peace, and some at war; some weeping, some laughing; some well, some sick; some coming into the world, some dying, etc." That was how they learned to respond to the call of Christ and to work for the establishment of his Kingdom. *(GC32 d. 4 n. 14)*

If we wish to continue to be faithful to this special character of our vocation and to the mission we have received from the Pope, we must "contemplate" our world as Ignatius did his, that we may hear anew the call of Christ dying and rising in the anguish and aspirations of men and women. *(GC32 d. 4 n. 19)*

13. Discernment

If we are to fulfill our mission, we must be faithful to that practice of communal apostolic discernment so central to "our way of proceeding," a practice rooted in the Exercises and Constitutions. This way of proceeding calls for a review of all our ministries, both traditional and new. *(GC33 d. 1 n. 39)*

14. Insertion

Too often we are insulated from any real contact with unbelief and with the hard, everyday consequences of injustice and oppression. As a result we run the risk of not being able to hear the cry for the Gospel as it is addressed to us by the men and women of our time. A deeper involvement with others in the world will therefore be a decisive test of our faith, of our hope, and of our apostolic charity. Are we ready, with discernment and with reliance on a community which is alive and apostolic, to bear witness to the Gospel in the painful situations where our faith and our hope are tested by unbelief and injustice? Are we ready to give ourselves to the demanding and serious study of theology, philosophy, and the human sciences, which are ever more necessary if we are to understand and try to resolve the problems of the world? To be involved in the world in this way is essential if we are to share our faith and our hope, and thus preach a Gospel that will respond to the needs and aspirations of our contemporaries. *(GC32 d. 4 n. 35)*

15. Openness and adaptation

We need a regular exposure to new situations of life and thought which oblige us to question our way of seeing and judging; a gradual assimilation of that apostolic pedagogy of St. Ignatius; a well-informed use of social and cultural analysis; and an inculturation which opens us to the newness of Jesus the Savior in the evolution of every people, and thereby prevents us from absolutizing our perceptions and actions. *(GC33 d. 1 n. 41)*

These arduous tasks which make up our mission "ad extra," like so many others, underscore for the whole Society the importance of a rigorously intellectual approach, in the general sense of "intellectual," as a specific aspect of the Jesuit contribution to the apostolate of the Lord's Church. Here the term is not limited to particular instruments of the intellectual apostolate, such as research and publication, higher education and scholarly editing. It refers, rather, to every apostolic activity of the Society which, for a greater service, must be suffused with the intellectual, its depth assured by solid studies and by the analysis of experience. *(Fr. Peter-Hans Kolvenbach, AR XIX 1076)*

16. Working with lay people

We must work more closely with lay men and women, respecting and supporting their distinct responsibility and vocation in the Church and in the world. Recent experience teaches us we can make a real contribution to forming a truly apostolic laity as well as receive from them great strength in our own vocation and for our mission. The renewal of Ignatian spirituality in certain fields (Exercises, Christian Life Communities, etc.) can help deepen this mutual collaboration. *(GC33 d. 1 n. 47)*

The 33rd General Congregation expressed the growing desire of the Society to associate lay people in its apostolic tasks in the Church today. This collaboration should not be promoted for reasons of pastoral tactics or on account of problems of numbers, but rather be inspired by the ecclesial vision which Vatican II would have us rediscover.

This very real aspect of "sentire cum Ecclesia" today supposes a faith incarnated in the Church, such as the Lord has wanted it and loved it: as His mystical body, as people of God and a communion in the Spirit. To become incarnated, this faith demands a large investment of time and of financial resources. *(Fr. Peter-Hans Kolvenbach, AR XIX 1086)*

17. *Solidarity with the poor*

The validity of our mission will also depend to a large extent on our solidarity with the poor. For though obedience sends us, it is poverty that makes us believable. So, together with many other religious congregations, we wish to make our own the Church's preferential option for the poor. This option is a decision to love the poor preferentially because there is a desire to heal the whole human family. Such love, like Christ's own, excludes no one, but neither does it excuse anyone from its demands. Directly or indirectly, this option should find some concrete expression in every Jesuit's life, in the orientation of our existing apostolic works, and in our choice of new ministries. "Only when we come to live out our consecration to the Kingdom in a communion that is for the poor, with the poor and against all forms of human poverty, material and spiritual, only then will the poor see that the gates of the Kingdom are open to them." *(GC33 d. 1 n. 48)*

C. Mission and Apostolates

18. *Our mission today*

Whether we consider the needs and aspirations of the men of our time, or reflect on the particular charism that founded our Society, or seek to learn what Jesus has in His heart for each and all of us, we are led to the identical conclusion that today the Jesuit is a man whose mission is to dedicate himself entirely to the service of faith and the promotion of justice, in a communion of life and work and sacrifice with the companions who have rallied round the same standard of the Cross and in fidelity to the Vicar of Christ, for the building up of a world at once more human and more divine. *(GC32 d. 2 n. 31)*

We confirm the Society's mission expressed by the 31st and 32nd General Congregations, particularly in the latter's Decrees 2 and 4, which are the application today of the Formula of the Institute and of our Ignatian charism. They express our mission today in profound terms offering insights which serve as guidelines for our future responses:

- the *integration* of the service of faith and the promotion of justice in one single mission;
- the *universality* of this mission in the various ministries in which we engage;
- the *discernment* needed to implement this mission;
- the *corporate* nature of this mission. *(GC33 d. 1 n. 38)*

The General Congregation emphasizes the importance of theological reflection, social action, education and the mass media. We should pursue these objectives not separately, in isolation, but as complementary factors of a single apostolate. *(GC32 d. 4 nn. 59, 61)*

19. Essential ministries

As we continue to respond to our mission, traditional apostolates take on fresh importance, while new needs and situations make new demands on us. The essential ministries of preaching the Gospel, fostering sacramental life, giving the Exercises, teaching, formation of the clergy, the work of catechetics, the promotion of Christian communities, and evangelizing those who have not yet heard of Christ—all should contribute to strengthening the faith that does justice. *(GC33 d. 1 n. 43)*

As we opened the 33rd General Congregation, we heard Pope John Paul II tell us: "The Church today expects the Society to contribute effectively to the implementation of the Second Vatican Council." Moreover, he repeated the mandate to confront the problem of atheism and cooperate in that profound renewal needed by the Church in a secularized world. He invited us to adapt our traditional apostolates to the different spiritual necessities of today, singling out the renewal of Christian life, the education of youth, the formation of the clergy, the study of philosophy and theology, research into humanistic and scientific cultures, and missionary activity. He encouraged us to pay particular attention to ecumenism, relations with other world religions, and the task of authentic inculturation. Finally, the Pope, speaking of our apostolate, again drew attention to the need to promote, within the Church's evangelizing action and in conformity with our priestly and religious Institute, "the justice, connected with world peace, which is an aspiration of all peoples." *(GC33 d. 1 n. 37)*

20. New needs

Among new needs and situations, certain problems call for special concern:

- the spiritual hunger of so many, particularly the young,

who search for meaning and values in a technological culture;

- attacks by governments on human rights through assassination, imprisonment, torture, the denial of religious freedom and political expression: all of which cause so many to suffer, some of them fellow Jesuits;

- the sad plight of millions of refugees searching for a permanent home, a situation brought to our special attention by Fr. Arrupe;

- discrimination against whole categories of human beings, such as migrants and racial or religious minorities;

- the unjust treatment and exploitation of women;

- public policies and social attitudes which threaten human life for the unborn, the handicapped and the aged;

- economic oppression and spiritual needs of the unemployed, of poor and landless peasants, and of workers, with whom many Jesuits, like our worker priests, have identified themselves in order to bring them the Good News. *(GC33 d. 1 n. 45)*

21. *For a more just and interdependent international social order*

As an international body, the Society of Jesus commits itself to that work which is the promotion of a more just world order, greater solidarity of rich countries with poor, and a lasting peace based on human rights and freedom. At this critical moment for the future of humanity, many Jesuits are cooperating more directly in the work for peace as intellectuals, organizers and spiritual leaders, and by their witness of non-violence. Following the example of recent Popes, we must strive for international justice and an end to an arms race that deprives the poor and threatens to destroy civilization. The evangelical call to be genuine peacemakers cautions us to avoid both naivety and fatalism. *(GC33 d. 1 n. 46)*

III. LIFE IN THE SPIRIT, A LIFE OF PRAYER

22. *Spiritual life*

The spiritual life is a participation in the life of the most holy Trinity dwelling within us so that we may be made conformed to the image of the Son of God, "so that He may be the firstborn among many brethren," for the glory of God.

This life involves the whole man and all his activities, by which he as a Christian corresponds to every impulse received from God. It does not consist only in individual acts of devotion, but ought to animate and direct our whole life, individual and community, together with all our relations to other persons and things. It is nourished and fostered by every grace by which God turns to us and communicates Himself to us, especially by His word and the sacraments of Christ. *(GC31 d. 13 n. 5.)*

23. *Union of action and prayer*

The Jesuit apostle goes from the Exercises, at once a school of prayer and of the apostolate, a man called by his vocation to be a contemplative in action. Our intimate union with Christ forges a union of our life of prayer and our life of apostolic work. Far from living two separate lives, we are strengthened and guided toward action in our prayer while our action in turn urges us to pray. Bringing salvation to men in word and deed through faith, hope, and love, we pray as we work and are invited to formal prayer that we may toil as true servants of God. In this interplay, praise, petition, thanksgiving, self-offering, spiritual joy, and peace join prayer and work to bring a fundamental unity into our lives. *(GC31 d. 14 n. 4)*

As a consequence, the General Congregation invites all Jesuits to strive, personally and communally, toward an even greater integration of our spiritual life and apostolate. Only to the extent that he is united to God so that he may be "led gladly by the divine hand," is a Jesuit "a man on a mission." In this way, he will learn to find God in all things, the God who is present in this world and its struggle between good and evil, between faith and unbelief, between the yearning for justice and peace and the growing reality of injustice and strife. But we cannot achieve this familiarity with God unless we set aside a regular time for personal prayer. *(GC33 d. 1 n. 11)*

- To possess today the vision and strength to fulfill our apostolic priorities and, in the process, to go generously against our natural inertia requires a docility to the Spirit that comes only as a gift—a gift that is the fruit of a humble search for the Spirit carried out in the depths of a life truly devoted to prayer.

- To preserve a proper balance among the religious, apostolic and priestly aspects of all our activities, particularly those of a markedly secular character, will only be possible if one has a living spiritual awareness that is shared with the brethren. *(Fr. Pedro Arrupe, AR XVI 956-957)*

24. *Necessity of personal prayer*

We are led to the absolute necessity of personal prayer for the familiarity with God which consists in finding Him in all things, and all things in Him. Christ Himself gave us an example of this. St. Ignatius urges it both in the Exercises and in the Constitutions. Our own personal experience confirms it. For while it is "in action" that we are called to be contemplative, this cannot obscure the fact that we *are* called to be contemplative. *(GC32 d. 11 n. 8)*

25. *Praying by inserting oneself in the People of God through the Word of God and the sacraments*

The people of God, in whom Christ shows us the way to the Father, are our people. Hence the prayer of every Christian is rooted in the prayer of the Church and flowers into liturgical action. Thus the celebration of the Eucharist is the center of the life of the apostolic religious community, bringing fraternal union to its perfection and blessing every apostolic endeavor with the waters of holiness. *(GC31 d. 14 n. 5)*

Our union with God in Christ is furthered not only by formal prayer, personal and communitarian, but also by the offering of Christ's sacrifice and the reception of his sacraments. Every Jesuit community is a faith community, and it is in the Eucharist that those who believe in Christ come together to celebrate their common faith. Our participation at the same table in the Body and Blood of Christ, more than anything else, makes us one companionship totally dedicated to Christ's mission in the world. *(GC32 d. 11 n. 12)*

Since it has pleased the Father to speak to men both in His Son, the Word Incarnate, and in many ways in Scripture, the Bible, a treasure bestowed by the Spouse on His Church to nourish and guide all men, is truly the ever-flowing font of prayer and renewal in religious life. In each of us, as the whole tradition of the Church attests, Holy Scripture becomes our saving word only when heard in prayer that leads to the submission of faith. *Lectio divina,* a practice dating back to the earliest days of religious life in the Church, supposes that the reader surrenders to God who is speaking and granting him a change of heart under the action of the two-edged sword of Scripture continually challenging to conversion. *(GC31 d. 14 n. 6)*

26. *Seeking familiarity with God through personal prayer*

Through mental prayer our individual lives receive clarity and meaning from the history of salvation, are set against the background of God's speaking to us, and hopefully are enriched with that freedom and spiritual discernment so necessary for the ministry of the Gospel. These reasons apply to all religious involved in the world today, which far too often ignores God. For these religious, formal prayer is a precious chance to see the unity of creation and to refer creation to the Father. Our own men, conscious of the special task of challenging atheism, find further apostolic significance in prayer as it fosters in us a sense of the living God and an encouragement of our faith. *(GC31 d. 14 n. 3)*

The Society counts on her men after their formation to be truly "spiritual men who have advanced in the way of Christ our Lord so as to run along this way," men who in this matter of prayer are led chiefly by that "rule which discerning love gives to each one," guided by the advice of his spiritual father and the approval of his superior.

All should recall that the prayer in which God communicates Himself more intimately is the better prayer, whether mental or even vocal, whether it be in meditative reading or in an intense feeling of love and self-giving. *(GC31 d. 14 n. 11)*

27. *Conditions for prayer*

To live a life of prayer, which in the Society is never separated from apostolic action, each of us must first deny himself so that, shedding his own personal inclinations, he may have that mind which is in Christ Jesus. For while on the one hand, prayer brings forth abnegation, since it is God who purifies man's heart by His presence, on the other, abnegation itself prepares the way for prayer, because only the pure of heart will see God. Progress in prayer is possible for those alone who continually try to put off their misguided affections to ready themselves to receive the light and grace of God. This continual conversion of heart "to the love of the Father of mercies" is intimately related to the repeated sacramental act of penance.

Self-denial, which disposes us for prayer and is one of its fruits, is not genuine unless amid the confusion of the world we try to keep our hearts at peace, our minds tranquil, and our desires restrained. *(GC31 d. 14 n. 8)*

This abnegation is required by the Spiritual Exercises: to divest ourselves of "self-love, self-will, and self-interest." It is only through detachment from all we have and are, that we can receive all from God in faith and give ourselves wholly to others in love. Without such an attitude we cannot present ourselves as interiorly free enough for the authentic service of Him who calls us. *(GC33 d. 1 n. 13)*

28. *Apostolic action based on prayer becomes union with God*

Inwardly strengthened and renewed by prayer and the sacraments, we are able to make apostolic action itself a form of union with God. Our service of the faith *[diakonia fidei]* and our service of men then become, not an interruption of that union but a continuation of it, a joining of our action with Christ's salvific action in history. Thus contemplation flows into action regularly, and we realize to some extent our ideal of being contemplatives "in action." *(GC32 d. 11 n. 13)*

IV. A LIFE CONSECRATED BY THE THREE VOWS

29. *Consecration*

Inserted by baptism into the Mystical Body of Christ, strengthened by confirmation with the power of the Holy Spirit, and consecrated into a royal priesthood and a holy people, we receive a more special consecration for the divine service in the Society of Jesus by the profession of the evangelical counsels, so that we may be able to bring forth richer fruits from the grace of baptism. *(GC31 d. 13 n. 2)*

30. *Liberation*

Not only our community life, but our religious vows are apostolic. If we commit ourselves until death to the evangelical counsels of poverty, chastity, and obedience, it is that we may be totally united to Christ and share His own freedom to be at the service of all who need us. In binding us, the vows set us free:

- free, by our vow of poverty, to share the life of the poor and to use whatever resources we may have not for our own security and comfort, but for service;

- free, by our vow of chastity, to be men for others, in friendship and communion with all, but especially with those who share our mission of service;

- free, by our vow of obedience, to respond to the call of Christ as made known to us by him whom the Spirit has placed over the Church, and to follow the lead of our superiors, especially our Father General, who has all authority over us *ad aedificationem. (GC32 d. 2 n. 20)*

31. *Prophetic role*

It is in this light that we are asked to renew our dedication to the properly apostolic dimension of our religious life. Our consecration to God is really a prophetic rejection of those idols which the world is always tempted to adore, wealth, pleasure, prestige, power. Hence our poverty, chastity, and obedience ought visibly to bear witness to this. Despite the inadequacy of any attempt to anticipate the Kingdom which is to come, our vows ought to show how by God's grace there can be, as the Gospel proclaims, a community among human beings which is based on sharing rather than on greed; on willing openness to all persons rather than on seeking after privileges of caste or class or race; on service rather than on domination and exploitation. The men and women of our time need a hope which is eschatological, but they also need to have some signs that its realization has already begun. *(GC32 d. 4 n. 16)*

A. Chastity

32. *An oblation to God*

Our vow of chastity consecrates a celibacy freely chosen for the sake of the Kingdom of God. By it, we offer an undivided heart to God, a heart capable of a self-giving in service approaching the freedom from self-interest with which God Himself loves all His creatures. *(GC32 d. 11 n. 26)*

33. *Its apostolic significance*

In our Society, chastity is essentially apostolic. It is not at all to be understood as directed exclusively to our personal sanctification. For, according to the whole intent of our Institute, we embrace chastity as a special source of spiritual fruitfulness in the world. Through it, full dominion of our energies, both bodily and spiritual, is retained for a prompter love and a more total apostolic availability towards all men.

Moreover, the profession of chastity for the sake of the kingdom of heaven is of itself a true preaching of the Gospel, for it reveals to all men how the kingdom of God prevails over every other earthly consideration, and it shows wonderfully at work in the Church the surpassing greatness of the force of Christ the King and the boundless power of the Holy Spirit. *(GC31 d. 16 n. 4)*

34. *To be perfectly observed*

God, pouring forth his charity in our hearts through the Holy Spirit, confers upon some in the Church the gift of consecrated chastity, a sign of charity and likewise a stimulus to it, whereby they may more easily devote themselves with an undivided heart to Him alone and to the service of His kingdom. Therefore, chastity "for the sake of the kingdom of heaven," to which by both His example and His calling Christ invites us, and which we as religious profess, following the lead of so many saints, should, as the Church repeatedly urges and as our founder expressly declares, be "perfectly observed" by us. *(GC31 d. 16 n. 1)*

35. *The sacrifices it requires and its fruitfulness*

Chastity vowed to God through celibacy implies and requires of us a sacrifice by which we knowingly and willingly forego entrance into that family relationship wherein husband and wife, parents and children, can in many ways, even psychologically, attain mutual fulfillment. Hence, our consecration to Christ involves a certain affective renunciation and a solitude of heart which form part of the cross offered to us by Jesus as we follow His footsteps, and which closely associate us with His paschal mystery and render us sharers of the spiritual fertility which flows from it. The vow of chastity, then, on the indispensable condition that it be accepted with a humble, joyous, and firm spirit as a gift from God, and be offered as a sacrifice to God, not only does not diminish our personality nor hamper human contacts and dialogue, but rather expands affectively, unites men fraternally, and brings them to a fuller charity. *(GC31 d. 16 n. 5)*

36. Necessity of friendship with Christ and familiarity with God

All should cultivate close friendship with Christ and familiarity with God, for in this world no one lives without love. But when our contemporaries question or fail to understand what our love is, we should offer them a fitting reply through the witness of a life of consecrated chastity, and at the same time with humble persevering prayer we should beg for ourselves and for our brothers the grace of a personal love for Christ.

For our Father Ignatius experienced this grace, so permeating his entire personality that he bound his brethren to himself as friends and by his personal affability led countless men and women to to God.

In the Spiritual Exercises he wished to urge the imploring of this grace, so that throughout the meditations and contemplations on the mysteries of the life, death, and resurrection of our Lord Jesus Christ, and in the application of the senses to them he would have us beg to know interiorly the Lord "who for me was made man, so that I may love Him the more, and follow Him more closely." *(GC31 d. 16 n. 8)*

37. Constant growth in chastity

All should keep in mind that love consecrated by chastity should constantly grow and approach the mature measure of the fullness of Christ. It is, consequently, not a gift bestowed once and for all, mature and complete, at the beginning of one's spiritual life, but such as by repeated decisions, perhaps serious ones, should steadily increase and become more perfect.

Thus the heart is more and more cleansed of affections not yet sufficiently understood, until the man adheres totally to Christ through love. *(GC31 d. 16 n. 8)*

38. Friendship and chastity

Such love of Jesus our Lord impels a person likewise to genuine human love for men and to true friendship. For chastity for the sake of the kingdom of heaven is safeguarded by fraternal friendship and in turn flowers forth in it. Hence also, we should regard as the precious apostolic fruit of ever more perfect love of friendship that mature, simple, anxiety-free dealing with men and women with whom and for whom we exercise our ministry for the building up of the body of Christ. *(GC31 d. 16 n. 8)*

B. Poverty

39. To imitate Christ poor and humble

Voluntary poverty in imitation of Christ is a sharing in that mystery revealed in the self-emptying of the very Son of God in the Incarnation. The Jesuit vocation to poverty draws its inspiration from the experience of St. Ignatius and the Spiritual Exercises and is specified by the Formula of the Institute and by the Constitutions. It is the charism of the Society to serve Christ poor and humble. The principle and foundation of our poverty, therefore, is found in a love of the Word made Flesh and crucified. *(GC32 d. 12 n. 2)*

Our first Fathers wanted to be "poor priests of Christ," not for purely philanthropic or pastoral reasons, but in response to the call of the Father inviting them to live together in a particular conformity to the Son, thus participating in His salvific mission. *(Fr. Pedro Arrupe, AR XV 279)*

Assuredly, we desire to bear witness, not to some ideology or virtue, but to Jesus Christ, and to the love and freedom He brings. It is in the persons of those who voluntarily embrace poverty that "the poor of Yahweh" may somehow live on. But above all, it is the Son of Man who lives in them, the Word of God born in the likeness of men. He, being found in the form of man, emptied himself and became humble, a servant, poor, hard-working, available to all, not claiming His own rights, yet supremely free. *(Fr. Pedro Arrupe, AR XV 277)*

40. Apostolic aspects

Religious poverty still calls to the following of Christ poor, but also to a following of Christ at work in Nazareth, identifying with the needy in His public life, the Christ of heartfelt compassion, responding to their needs, eager to serve them. *(GC32 d. 12 n. 4)*

The situation of the poor, who live in a world where unjust structures force the greater part of the human family to exist in dehumanizing conditions, should be a constant reminder to us that God takes the part of the poor, according to that salvific design revealed in Jesus Christ who "came to proclaim the Good News to the poor." In recent years, the Church has summoned us to a greater solidarity with the poor and to more effective attempts to attack the very causes of mass poverty. *(GC33 d. 1 n. 26)*

Jesuits will be unable to hear the "cry of the poor" unless they have greater personal experience of the miseries and distress of the poor. It will be difficult for the Society everywhere to forward effectively the cause of justice and human dignity if the greater part of her ministry identifies her with the rich and powerful, or is based on the "security of possession, knowledge, and power." Our life will be no "witness to a new eternal life won by Christ's redemption or to a resurrected state and the glory of the heavenly kingdom," if individually and corporately, Jesuits are seen to be attached to earthly things, even apostolic institutions, and to be dependent on them. Our communities will have no meaning or sign value for our times, unless by their sharing of themselves and all they possess, they are clearly seen to be communities of charity and of concern for each other and all others. *(GC32 d. 12 n. 5)*

Every Jesuit, no matter what his ministry, is called "to preach in poverty," according to the *sacra doctrina* of the Two Standards, and this poverty has a spiritual power not to be measured in human terms. Apostolic efficiency and apostolic poverty are two values to be held in an ongoing tension, and this is a rule for apostolic institutes as well as for individuals. The expedience of retaining rich and powerful institutions, requiring great capital outlay, is to be weighed prudently and spiritually. Since these institutions are but means, the attitude of the Society should be that of the Third Class of Men, and according to the rule of *tantum quantum,* fully as ready to abandon as to retain, to the greater service of God. The faithful practice of religious poverty is apostolic, too, in its contempt of personal gain, which commends the Gospel and frees the apostle to preach it in all its integrity. It is apostolic, finally, in that communities which are really poor, by their simplicity and fraternal union, proclaim the beatitudes, "manifesting to all believers the presence of heavenly goods already possessed here below." *(GC32 d. 12 n. 9)*

41. To live in common with nothing of one's own

It is on the basis of our religious poverty as specifically apostolic and because of the witness to truly liberal charity to which our vocation urges us, that we share in common not only our lives and our efforts, but also our material goods. Fraternal charity among apostles expresses itself particularly by this sharing and by the spontaneous care for equality, as much as this is possible. *(Fr. Pedro Arrupe, AR XV 280)*

42. Our poverty must be sincere

Our profession of poverty should be sincere, so that the manner of our life corresponds to this profession. The Society really intends to answer the demands of this real, not pretended, poverty. *(GC31 d. 18 n. 7)*

It is the poor who call upon the Society of Jesus to follow a Christ who is poor and who brings Good News to the poor (GC32 d. 2 n. 28). Especially in letters coming from countries where misery and injustice are rampant the question is posed whether the face of Christ which we contemplate in our personal prayer is, in fact, the whole Christ. Might not our prayer be that of the second class of men *(Sp. Ex.* 154) who are always trying to reconcile the face of Christ with the things they want to look at, "so that God may come to what they desire"? It is only when contemplation makes us one with the poor Christ, Himself one with the most deprived, that we make essential about-faces in our manner and style of living, and in what and whom we identify with, and in our apostolic choices (GC32 d. 4 nn. 46-47). *(Fr. Peter-Hans Kolvenbach, Jesuit Life in the Spirit, 26 March 1989)*

Religious poverty should try hard to limit rather than expand consumption. It is not possible to love poverty or to experience its mysterious consolations, without some knowledge of its actuality. The need for reform is so frequently evident that no person or community may decline this examination. *(GC32 d. 12 n. 7)*

43. Poverty, work, salary, gratuity

The witness of our poverty today most aptly shines forth in our practice and spirit of work undertaken for the kingdom of God and not for temporal gain. This poverty should be filled with activity, by which we resemble men who must earn their daily bread; it should be equitable and just, ordered in the first place to giving each one his due; finally, it should be generous, so that by our labor we may help our poorer houses, our works, and the poor. *(GC31 d. 18 n. 8)*

Manifestly, our spirit of poverty is not seriously carried into practice unless each one of us realistically and methodically employs his energies and time, even his leisure and holidays which law, scholastic ordinations, and other sources allow; and unless each one imposes on himself a life of dedicated work, reasonable hygiene or care of bodily health, and personal self-discipline. On all these the rich fruits of our energies are dependent. But the poverty of Christ and His disciples is lived out in any kind of activities, contemplative or intellectual, in ministries strictly spiritual as well as in other occupations necessary or useful—and that whether our service is an occasion of remuneration or gifts or whether nothing of this sort follows. *(Fr. Pedro Arrupe, AR XV 283-284)*

In our choice of ministries, the spirit of gratuity proper to our Institute should be carefully kept in mind so that "the exercise of those ministries which according to our tradition were provided gratuitously should not be abandoned too easily." *(GC33 d. 1 n. 27)*

44. *Poverty and sharing as service to the poor*

Our poverty should become a sign of our charity in that by our lack we enrich others. Nothing should be our own so that all things may be common in Christ. Communities themselves, renouncing their own advantage, should be united to each other by the bond of solidarity. Finally, the parts of the Society should freely become poorer so that they may serve the whole body of the Society. And the bond of charity should not be restricted only to Jesuits, for all men are related to the Mystical Body of Christ. Charity should always crown the obligations of justice by which we are bound in a special way to those who are poor and to the common good. *(GC31 d. 18 n. 9)*

The Society, facing a world in which a large part of

mankind lies wounded and despoiled, moved by the love of the Good Samaritan, and conscious of its universal vocation, should subject its apostolate to examination, to see how it may more fully turn itself to those who are abandoned, "to evangelize the poor, to heal the crushed in heart." *(GC31 d. 18 n. 11)*

The Church regards the ministry of justice as integral to the contemporary practice of poverty. Such commitment is everywhere needed, but in many places it is a very condition of credibility for the Society and for the Church. The insertion of communities among the poor so that Jesuits may work for them and with them, or at least may acquire some experience of their condition, is a testimony of love of the poor and of poverty to which the Church encourages religious. *(GC32 d. 12 n. 10)*

45. *Interior disposition and effective experience*

All should remember that no community form of poverty or any outward profession of it will be genuinely Christian unless it is inspired by a highly personal sentiment of the heart, that is, by a spiritual poverty, drawn from a close and constant union with the incarnate Word of God. Therefore, there is a broad field of personal responsibility in which each can more perfectly live his calling to poverty and, within the limits of the common good, express it with discerning love by living more frugally, under the guidance of superiors. *(GC31 d. 18 n. 10)*

This is the desire of the Congregation, this its prayer to God for the Society, a poverty profoundly renewed:

- simple in community expression and joyous in the following of Christ;
- happy to share with each other and with all;
- apostolic in its active indifference and readiness for any service;
- inspiring our selection of ministries and turning us to those most in need;

- spiritually effective, proclaiming Jesus Christ in our way of life and in all we do.

The authenticity of our poverty after all does not consist so much in the lack of temporal goods, as in the fact that we live, and are seen to live, from God and for God, sincerely striving for the perfection of that ideal which is the goal of the spiritual journey of the Exercises: "Give me only Your love and Your grace, and I am rich enough, and ask for nothing more." *(GC32 d. 12 n. 14)*

C. Obedience

46. *Mission and obedience*

Impelled by love of Christ, we embrace obedience as a distinctive grace conferred by God on the Society through its founder, whereby we may be united the more surely and constantly with God's salvific will, and at the same time be made one in Christ among ourselves. For the Society of Jesus is a group of men who seek close union with Christ and a share in the saving mission which He realized through obedience unto death. Christ invited us to take part in such a mission when, bearing His cross, he told St. Ignatius at La Storta, "I will that you serve Us." Through obedience, then, strengthened by vow, we follow "Jesus Christ still carrying His cross in the Church militant, to whom the eternal Father gave us as servants and friends, that we may follow Him with our cross" and be made His companions in glory. Now through the vow of obedience our Society becomes a more fit instrument of Christ in His Church, unto the assistance of souls, for God's greater glory. *(GC31 d. 17 n. 2)*

47. Obeying superiors for the love of Christ

The first Fathers of the Society held the unshaken conviction that "they had no other head than Christ Jesus, whom alone they hoped to serve," and they solemnly sanctioned this fact in the Formula of the Institute, affirming that they wanted "to serve the Lord alone." In the same Formula, however, they already expressly declared that "they are serving the Lord alone and the Church His spouse, under the Roman Pontiff," understanding that they offer obedience to Christ Himself when they obey the visible head of the Church. Moreover, in the deliberations of the first Fathers, all decided unanimously that they should obey not only the Vicar of Christ, but also the superior chosen from among them, "so that we can more sincerely and with greater praise and merit fulfill through all things the will of God." St. Ignatius repeatedly states this, that every superior is to be obeyed "in the place of Christ and for the love of Christ." *(GC31 d. 17 n. 3)*

Just as the Son of God "emptied himself, taking the form of a servant, being born in the likeness of men"; just as he "humbled himself and became obedient unto death, even death on a cross," so also do members of the Society from love for Christ and to gain souls, "offer the full dedication of their own will as a sacrifice of self to God." Thus they bind themselves entirely to God, beloved above all, and by a new and special title dedicate and consecrate themselves to His service and honor, bearing witness to the new freedom whereby Christ has made us free. *(GC31 d. 17 n. 12)*

48. Complete and sincere obedience

Obedience is to be offered by all promptly, cheerfully, and in a supernatural spirit, as to Christ. In this spirit, all should make their own the superior's command in a personal, responsible way, and with all diligence "bring to the execution of commands and the discharge of assignments entrusted to them the resources of their minds and wills, and their gifts of nature and grace," "realizing that they are giving service to the upbuilding of Christ's body according to God's design." Hence, not just any sort of obedience is expected of us, but an obedience full and generous, of the intellect, too, insofar as possible, rendered in a spirit of faith, humility, and modesty. *(GC31 d. 17 n. 9)*

Our holy Father St. Ignatius desired that we should all excel in the virtue of obedience. Accordingly, with all our force and energy we should strive to obey, first, the Sovereign Pontiff, and then the superiors of the Society, "not only in matters of obligation, but also in others, even at the mere hint of the superior's will, apart from any express command." We are to respond with perfect obedience in all things where there is not manifestly any sin. Nor may a subject refuse to obey because he thinks it would be better to do other things, or because he believes he is led along lines by the inspiration of the Holy Spirit. *(GC31 d. 17 n. 10)*

49. Duty of responsibility

Obedience is the ordinary means by which God's will is made clear to the members of the Society. However, it does not take away, but rather by its very nature and perfection supposes in the subject the obligation of personal responsibility and the spirit of ever seeking what is better. Consequently the subject can, and sometimes should, set forth his own reasons and proposals to the superior. Such a way of acting is not opposed to perfect obedience, but is reasonably required by it, in order that by an effort common to both superior and subject the divine will may more easily and surely be found. *(GC31 d. 17 n. 11)*

50. Meaning of "obedience of judgment"

Obedience of judgment does not mean that our intellect is bereft of its proper role, and that one should assent to the superior's will against reason, rejecting the evidence of truth. For the Jesuit, employing his own intelligence, confirmed by the unction of the Holy Spirit, makes his own the will and judgment of superiors, and with his intellect endeavors to see their orders as more conformed to the will of God. He diverts his attention from a fretful consideration of the opposite reasons, and directs it solely to positive reasons intrinsic to the matter or to motives which transcend this order, namely, values of faith and charity. For practical matters are at issue, in which almost always there remains some doubt as to what is most fitting and more pleasing to God. Theoretical certitude or very high probability about the objective superiority of a given solution is not to be awaited before a superior can authoritatively impose it; nor are the reasons for a course of action always and everywhere to be given the subject that he may devote himself wholeheartedly to the goals and works assigned to him. For the final reason for religious obedience is the authority of the superior. Trust is to be placed in Christ, who by means of obedience wishes to lead the Church and the Society to the ends He proposes. *(GC31 d. 17 n. 11)*

51. Spiritual government

After the example of Christ, whose place he holds, the superior should exercise his authority in a spirit of service, desiring not to be ministered unto but to serve. While he maintains sincere interior reverence, he should exercise simplicity in his way of speaking, so that the friendly concord of Christ with His apostles may come to view.

Hence government in the Society should always be spiritual, conscious before God of personal responsibility and of the obligation to rule one's subjects as sons of God and with regard for the human personality, strong where it needs to be, open and sincere. Superiors should reckon their direction of Jesuits, both as a community and as individuals, more important than any other tasks to be done.

In the exercise of authority, however, the gift of discretion or of discerning love is most desirable. To acquire this virtue, so necessary for good government, the superior should first of all be free from ill-ordered affections and be closely united and familiar with God. Besides, he ought to know thoroughly our ways of acting, according to our Institute. Keeping in view, then, our end, which is none other than the greater service of God and the good of those who engage in this course of life, he should command the things which he believes will contribute towards attaining the end proposed by God and the Society, maintaining withal due respect for persons, places, times, and other circumstances. *(GC31 d. 17 nn. 4-5)*

52. *Familiar exchange between superior and companions: The account of conscience*

This truly spiritual government, whereby Jesuits are directed by superiors with discerning love rather than through external laws, supposes communication between the two which is as far as possible plain and open. The superior should endeavor to make his mind clearly known to his brothers and understood by them; and he should take care that they, according to the nature and importance of the matter and as their own talents and duties require, share more fully in his knowledge and concern both for the personal and community life of Jesuits and for their apostolic labors. The religious, for his part, should try to make himself known, with his gifts and limitations, his desires, difficulties, and ideas, through a confiding, familiar and candid colloquy, about which the superior is held to strict secrecy. In this way an account of conscience is obtained which is sincere and open in form, and not reduced to a formal, periodic inquiry about actions already performed. That kind of friendly and confidential conversation, one that is frankly spiritual and aims at promoting the apostolic objective of our vocation and the religious sanctification of the apostle, will constitute the dialogue that is fundamental and essential for the wholesome progress of our Society. Hence it is the mind of the Congregation that the account of conscience in its proper sense should remain and be strengthened as a general practice. But it is charity which should inspire it, as St. Ignatius wishes, with any obligation under pain of sin always precluded. *(GC31 d. 17 n. 8)*

53. *Consultation with many . . . and sometimes with all*

But in order that he may more easily discover the will of God, the superior should have at hand able advisers and should often consult them. He should also use the services of experts in reaching decisions on complex matters. This will the more easily enable members of the Society to be convinced that their superior knows how, wants, and is able, to govern them well in the Lord. Besides, since all who work together in God's service are under the influence of the Holy Spirit and His grace, it will be well in the Lord to use their ideas and advice so as to understand God's will better. *(GC31 d. 17 n. 6)*

Superiors in the Society should readily and often ask for and listen to the counsel of their brethren, of a few or of many, or even of all gathered together, according to the importance and nature of the matter. Superiors should gratefully welcome suggestions which their fellow Jesuits offer spontaneously, with a single desire of greater spiritual good and the better service of God, but the duty of the superior himself to decide and enjoin what ought to be done remains intact. *(GC31 d. 17 n. 6)*

54. *Role of the superior in community discernment*

What is the role of the superior in communitarian discernment? It is, first, to develop, as far as he can, the requisite disposition for it; second, to decide when to convoke the community for it, and clearly to define its object; third, to take active part in it as the bond of union within the community and as the link between the community and the Society as a whole; and, finally, to make the final decision in the light of the discernment, but freely, as the one to whom both the grace and the burden of authority are given. For in our Society the discerning community is not a deliberative or capitular body but a consultative one, whose object, clearly understood and fully accepted, is to assist the superior to determine what course of action is for God's greater glory and the service of men. *(GC32 d. 11 n. 24)*

55. *Subsidiarity and the superior's trust in his companions*

It is also advantageous to the Society that the superior leave much in his orders to the prudence of his brothers, making liberal use of the principle of subsidiarity. To the extent that they make the spirit of the Society their own, especially if they are men long proven in humility and self-denial, individuals are to be allowed suitable freedom in the Lord. And finally, the universal good itself will sometimes demand that, in the manner of urging what has been commanded, account be taken also of human frailty. *(GC31 d. 17 n. 7)*

V. UNITY AND COMMUNITY

56. Union and community, values of the apostolic life

The sense of community evolved gradually in the infant Society. The first members, "friends in the Lord," after they had offered themselves and their lives to Christ the Lord and given themselves to His vicar on earth that he might send them where they could bear more fruit, decided to associate themselves into one body so that they might make stronger and more stable every day their union and association which was begun by God, "making ourselves into one body, caring for and understanding one another for the greater good of souls." Similarly they agreed later to give their obedience to some superior "so that they might better and more carefully fulfill their first desires to do the divine will in all things," and gain greater internal cohesion, stability, and apostolic efficacy. *(GC31 d. 19 n. 1)*

The dispersal imposed on us today by our vocation as Jesuits makes it imperative that we strengthen and renew the ties that bind us together as members of the same Society. That is why it is so important that our communities be apostolic communities, and it is the primary responsibility of the local superior to see to it that his community approach this ideal as closely as possible. Each one of us should be able to find in his community—in shared prayer, in converse with his brethren, in the celebration of the Eucharist—the spiritual resources he needs for the apostolate. The community should also be able to provide him with a context favorable to apostolic discernment. *(GC32 d. 4 nn. 62-63)*

The Jesuit community is a community of discernment. The missions on which Jesuits are sent, whether corporately or individually, do not exempt us from the need of discerning together in what manner and by what means such missions are to be accomplished. *(GC32 d. 2 n. 19)*

What St. Ignatius says about the need for union of minds and hearts among us was never more true than now: "The more difficult it is for members of this congregation to be united with their head and among themselves, since they are so scattered among the faithful and among unbelievers in diverse regions of the world, the more ought means to be sought for that union. For the Society cannot be preserved, or governed, or, consequently, attain the end it seeks for the greater glory of God, unless its members are united among themselves and with their head." *(GC32 d. 11 n. 4)*

57. *Our community: local, province and the whole body of the Society*

The particular local community to which a Jesuit may belong at any given moment is, for him, simply a concrete—if, here and now, a privileged—expression of this worldwide brotherhood. *(GC32 d. 2 n. 16)*

The apostolic body of the Society to which we belong should not be thought of just in terms of the local community. We belong to a province, which should itself constitute an apostolic community in which discernment and coordination of the apostolate on a larger scale than at the local level can and should take place. Moreover, the province is part of the whole Society, which also forms one single apostolic body and community. It is at this level that the over-all apostolic decisions and guidelines must be made and worked out, decisions and guidelines for which we should all feel jointly responsible. *(GC32 d. 4 n. 68)*

58. *A genuinely religious community*

Community in the Society of Jesus takes its origin from the will of the Father joining us into one, and is constituted by the active, personal, united striving of all members to fulfill the divine will, with the Holy Spirit impelling and guiding us individually through responsible obedience to a life which is apostolic in many ways. It is a community of men who are called by Christ to live with Christ, to fulfill the work of Christ in themselves and among men. *(GC31 d. 19 n. 2)*

59. *Fraternal community,* koinonia

A *communitas ad dispersionem,* but also a *koinonia,* a sharing of goods and life, with the Eucharist at its center: the sacrifice and sacrament of the Deed of Jesus, who loved his own to the end. And each member of every Jesuit community is ever mindful of what St. Ignatius says about love, that it consists in sharing what one has, what one is, with those one loves. When we speak of having all things in common, that is what we mean. *(GC32 d. 2 n. 18)*

By forming in this way a community of brothers, we bear witness to the presence of God among men: God who, as Trinity, is, beyond all imagining, a community of Love; God who, made Man, established with men an everlasting covenant. *(GC32 d. 11 n. 15)*

60. *Conditions of union in the body of the Society and in our communities*

Where, then, do we begin? We begin with the Ignatian insight that the unity of an apostolic body such as ours must be based on the union of each and all with God in Christ. For if we have come together as a companionship, it is because we have, each of us, responded to the call of the Eternal King. *(GC32 d. 11 n. 6)*

The union of minds of the members among themselves and with their head, leading to personal holiness and at the same time to apostolic activity, flows from a love for our God and Lord, Jesus Christ, and is sustained and governed by the same love. *(GC31 d. 19 n. 3)*

This union of hearts will be effected mainly by "the bond of obedience, which unites individuals with their superiors, and these among themselves and with the provincials, and all with Father General." *(GC31 d. 17 n. 13)*

Times of stress and trial that might threaten our fraternal communion from time to time can become moments of grace, which confirm our dedication to Christ and make that dedication credible. For, obviously, there is a reciprocal relationship between the religious vows and community life. The living of the vows promotes and strengthens community life; community life, in turn, if truly fraternal, helps us to be faithful to our vows. *(GC32 d. 11 n. 25)*

61. *Communication in our community life*

The following are increasingly necessary for community life in the Society of Jesus: exchange of information in the community, frequent consultation, delegation, collaboration of every kind, transcending every sort of individualism. A certain order of life which is determined by the conditions of life and work proper to each community, creating those exterior and interior conditions of silence, recollection, and peace of mind, which are so useful for personal study, reflection, and especially prayer.

The more clearly the members recognize that they are connected with the whole life and apostolate of the Society, the more community life will become psychologically and spiritually richer. *(GC31 d. 19 n. 5)*

Fraternal communication within the community can take many forms according to different needs and circumstances. But its basic presupposition is, at the human level, sincerity and mutual trust and, at the level of grace, those gifts of God with which our companionship began and by which it is maintained. *(GC32 d. 11 n. 19)*

Certain features of our Ignatian heritage can be given a

communitarian dimension; provided, of course, the personal practice for which they were originally intended is not abandoned. For instance, the examination of conscience could, at times, be made a shared reflection on the community's fidelity to its apostolic mission. Similarly, fraternal correction and personal dialogue with the superior can usefully become a community review of community life style. *(GC32 d. 11 n. 20)*

Community spiritual interchange can, under certain conditions, become communitarian discernment. This is something quite distinct from the usual community dialogue. It is "a corporate search for the will of God by means of a shared reflection on the signs which point where the Spirit of Christ is leading," and the method to follow in such communitarian discernment is analogous to that which St. Ignatius teaches for the making of a personal decision on a matter of importance.

There are prerequisites for a valid communitarian discernment. On the part of the individual member of the community, a certain familiarity with the Ignatian rules for the discernment of spirits, derived from actual use; a determined resolution to find the will of God for the community whatever it may cost; and, in general, the dispositions of mind and heart called for and cultivated in the First and Second Weeks of the Exercises. On the part of the community as such, a clear definition of the matter to be discerned, sufficient information regarding it, and "a capacity to convey to one another what each one really thinks and feels." *(GC32 d. 11 nn. 21-22; Fr. Peter-Hans Kolvenbach, AR XIX 700-715)*

VI. PRESERVATION AND INCREASE OF THIS BODY

62. *Vocations*

The General Congregation earnestly invites all Jesuits to take to heart the task of attracting vocations to the Society, especially by prayer and the example of their lives as individuals and in community. *(GC33 d. 1 n. 22)*

The promotion of vocations involves, certainly, a specialized work to be accomplished by those whom the Provincial assigns to it. But more broadly, it requires a mobilization of the whole body of the Province, possessor of a vocation which can attract others if it is lived in all its truth. Here is an area where every Jesuit and every community needs renewal. More than ever, considering the world and the culture in which they grow to maturity, young people of today need to meet persons who help them effectively in the encounter with Jesus Christ, and in the discovery of the call which echoes in their life.

Let us then pray for vocations. Let us force ourselves to renew and deepen our contact with young people. Let us be as transparent as possible so that they can see the grace which makes of us companions of Jesus. *(Fr. Peter-Hans Kolvenbach, AR XIX 274)*

63. *Formation*

Our formation must prepare witnesses and ministers of the faith who, as members of the Society, are ready to be sent for the greater service of the Church into situations which are characterized by uncertainty. Their formation must make our men capable of dialogue with others, capable of confronting the cultural problems of our day. For these are the circumstances under which they must labor to promote the spiritual growth of mankind according to the tradition of the Society. *(GC32 d. 6 n. 6)*

To respond to this apostolic vision, the whole formation of our members must be understood and promoted as a process of integration into the apostolic body of the Society. *(GC32 d. 6 n. 7)*

64. *The brothers*

For its part the Congregation, while sharing the concern expressed in many parts of the world, once again proclaims and affirms the incalculable value of the brothers' vocation, through which the Society develops its mission to the full. The Society needs the brothers, first of all for themselves and then for their labors, for the sake of both its communities and its apostolates. They share in the same religious commitment and take on work that is complementary to that characteristic of priests, thus effectively helping the Society to achieve its one and only goal. Being all members of the same body, we complete and enrich one another so that we can imitate the way of life offered by the Son of God to the disciples who followed Him. This is why the Congregation considers that the absence of brothers is a serious defect and that we cannot remain satisfied with the present situation. *(GC33 d. 1 n. 17)*

65. *Continuing formation*

Especially in our times, when everything is subject to such rapid change and evolution, and when new questions and new knowledge, both in theology and in other branches of learning, are constantly developing, a truly contemporary apostolate demands of us a process of permanent and continuing formation. Thus formation is never ended, and our "first" formation must be seen as the beginning of this continuing process. *(GC32 d. 6 n. 18)*

Closely following the Church, which, in liturgical renewal, biblical and theological reflection, and attention to the changing conditions of the times, is led by the Holy Spirit to complement the wisdom of antiquity by means of new developments, all, even those who have already completed their formation, should strive constantly to draw from these sources renewal for their own spiritual lives. Their apostolic activity will thus be enabled to answer more effectively the needs of the Church and of men. *(GC31 d. 8 n. 46)*

Continuing formation is achieved especially through a constant evaluation of and reflection on one's apostolate, in the light of faith and with the help of one's apostolic community. It also needs the cooperation of our professors and experts, whose theory can shed light on our praxis, even while they themselves are led to more profound reflection by the apostolic experience of their fellow Jesuits. This kind of communication will also assist the integration of the young into the apostolic life of the province, and the contact between formation and the apostolate will profit the whole Society. *(GC32 d. 6 n. 19)*

PART THREE

PRACTICAL RULES

Sacramental and Personal Prayer

1. Because "the work of our redemption is constantly carried on in the mystery of the Eucharistic Service," all of our members should consider daily celebration of the Eucharist as the center of their religious and apostolic life. Concelebrations are encouraged, especially on days when the community can more easily gather together. *(GC32 d. 11 n. 35)*

2. Our priests should try to pray the Divine Office attentively and at a suitable time. It is a wonderful song of praise, which is truly Christ's prayer to the Father, made through His body, the Church. *(GC31 d. 14 n. 10)*

3. In order to respond to the interior need for familiarity with God, we should all spend some time each day in personal prayer. Therefore, for those still in formation, "the Society retains the practice of an hour and a half as the time for prayer, Mass, and thanksgiving. Each man should be guided by his spiritual father as he seeks that form of prayer in which he can best advance in the Lord. The judgment of superiors is normative for each." For others, "our rule of an hour's prayer is to be adapted so that each Jesuit, guided by his superiors, takes into account his particular circumstances and needs, in the light of a discerning love." *(GC32 d. 11 n. 36)*

4. For the faithful fulfillment of their apostolic vocation both

communities and individuals should cherish daily converse with Christ the Lord in visiting the Blessed Sacrament. *(GC31 d. 14 n. 15)*

5. The time order of the community should include some brief daily common prayer and at times, in a way that is appropriate for each apostolic community, a longer period for prayer and prayerful discussion. Shared prayer, days of recollection, and the Spiritual Exercises in common are recognized as fruitful means for increasing union. *(GC32 d. 11 n. 37)*

6. Our entire apostolic life should be examined with the spiritual discernment proper to the Exercises. One means available to us is the daily examination of conscience, which was recommended by St. Ignatius so that we might be continually guided by the practice of spiritual discernment. *(GC32 d. 11 n. 38)*

7. Since we need the grace of continual conversion of heart "to the love of the Father of mercies" that the purity and freedom of our lives in God's service might increase, all should frequent the Sacrament of Reconciliation. We should also willingly participate in communal penitential services and strive to promote the spirit of reconciliation in our communities. *(GC32 d. 11 n. 39)*

8. Every Jesuit, especially during formation but also when he is engaged in an active apostolate, should make every effort to have a spiritual director with whom he can speak frequently and openly. *(GC32 d. 11 n. 40)*

9. The Spiritual Exercises are a privileged means for achieving renovation and union in the Society and for revitalizing our apostolic mission. They should be made by all every year, according to the method of St. Ignatius, for eight successive days. Adaptations may be allowed because of particular circumstances; the Provincial is to be the judge of the merits of each case. The circumstances of the annual retreat (such as

silence, recollection, a location removed from ordinary work) should be managed in such a way that the Jesuit is able truly to renew his spiritual life through frequent and uninterrupted familiar conversation with God. *(GC32 d. 11 n. 42 and GC31 d. 14 n. 16)*

10. The cult of the Sacred Heart of Jesus and the devotion to our Lady retain their value and it is fitting that we make use of these forms of spirituality, taking into account the differences which exist in various parts of the world. *(GC32 d. 11 n. 43)*

Chastity

11. To attain the perfect liberty of chaste love, besides familiarity with God, all the supernatural and natural helps available should be used. *(GC31 d. 16 n. 8c)*

12. Among these, those contribute more to the faithful fulfillment of one's oblation of chastity which are positive, such as probity of life, generous dedication to one's assigned task, great desire for the glory of God, zeal for solid virtues and spiritual concerns, openness and simplicity in activity and in consulting with superiors, rich cultural attainments, spiritual joy, and above all true charity. *(GC31 d. 16 n. 8c)*

13. Mindful of solitude of heart and of our frailty, we cannot forget the ascetical norms which the Church and the Society in their wide experience maintain and which the dangers against chastity require. *(GC31 d. 16 n. 8d)*

14. Sustained by the grace of God, we should generously and strenuously devote ourselves to apostolic labor and know how to participate with moderation in the human contacts which our ministry involves, our visits and recreations, our reading and study of problems, our attendance at shows, and use of what is pleasurable, so that the testimony of our consecration to God will shine forth inviolate. *(GC31 d. 16 n. 8e)*

15. Superiors should lovingly endeavor to lead back those whom they see or sense to be drawing away from the community. All Jesuits should be prepared to cooperate with superiors in their solicitude, discreetly but in good time making known to them the difficulties and temptations of their brothers. *(GC31 d. 16 n. 9e)*

Poverty and Common Life

16. Independence from the community in acquisition or expenditure, a vice with manifold disguises, cannot be tolerated. Every Jesuit must contribute to the community everything he receives by way of remuneration, stipend, alms, gift, or in any other way. He receives from the community alone everything he needs. In the same way, by cheerfully and gratefully accepting the community's standard of living, each undertakes to support his brothers in their efforts to live and love poverty. Those who are unwilling to observe this double law of common life, separate themselves from the fraternity of the Society in spirit if not in law. A peculium is not admitted among us. *(GC32 d. 12 n. 8 and Fr. Arrupe, AR XV 486 [n. 4])*

17. The standard of living of our houses should not be higher than that of a family of slender means whose providers must work hard for its support. The concrete exigencies of such a standard are to be discerned by individuals and communities in sincere deliberation with their superiors. It should look to food and drink, lodging and clothing, but also and perhaps especially to travel, recreation, use of automobiles, and of villas, vacations, etc. Some should scrutinize their leisure, sometimes such as hardly the rich enjoy. *(GC32 d. 12 n. 7)*

18. The standard of living with regard to food, clothing, and furniture should be common to all so that, poor in fact and in spirit, differences may be avoided as far as possible. This does not prevent each one from having what is necessary for his

work with the permission of the superior. *(GC31 d. 19 n. 7d)*

19.   Communities may not accumulate capital but must dispose of any annual surplus, according to a provincial plan which will look to the needs of communities, of apostolates, and of the poor. *(GC32 d. 12 n. 12)*

20.   There is a broad field of personal responsibility in which each can more perfectly live his calling to poverty and, within the limits of the common good, express it with discerning love by living more frugally, under the guidance of superiors. *(GC31 d. 18 n. 10)*

Obedience

21.   The Society's members, consecrated to a mission under obedience, should leave to their superiors the full and completely free disposition of themselves, desiring to be guided not by their own judgment and will, but by that indication of the divine will which is offered to us through obedience. Obedience is to be offered by all promptly, cheerfully, and in a supernatural spirit, as to Christ. *(GC31 d. 17 n. 9)*

22.   Obedience tests our sense of responsibility and our sense of initiative since it requires that all should make their own the command and intention of the superior in a personal, responsible way, and with all diligence "bring to the execution of commands and the discharge of assignments entrusted to them the resources of their minds and wills and their gifts of nature and grace," "realizing that they are giving service to the upbuilding of Christ's body according to God's design." *(Ibid.)*

23.   The subject can, and sometimes should, set forth his own reasons and proposals to the superior. *(GC31 d. 17 n. 11)*

Vowed obedience, whether in humdrum or in heroic matters, is always an act of faith and freedom whereby the religious recognizes and embraces the will of God manifested to him by one who has authority to send him in the name of Christ. He does not necessarily have to understand why he is being sent. *(GC32 d. 11 n. 31)*

24. The account of conscience is of great importance for the spiritual governance of the Society, and its practice is to be esteemed and cultivated. Therefore, all should give an account of conscience to their superiors, according to the norm and spirit of the Society. In addition, the relationship between superiors and their brethren in the Society should be such as to encourage the account of conscience and conversation about spiritual matters. *(GC32 d. 11 n. 46)*

Community

25. A community of Jesuits should above all be a true faith community, whose strongest bond is that of charity. It is for this reason that we embrace in the same love both God and those to whom He has confided the same salvific mission. *(GC32 d. 11 n. 41)*

26. All Jesuits, even those who must live apart because of the demands of their apostolate or for other justifiable reasons, should take an active part in the life of some community. To the extent that the bond with a community and its superior is more than merely juridical, that union of minds and hearts which is so desirable will be kept intact. *(GC32 d. 11 n. 44)*

27. Every community of the Society should have its own superior. *(GC32 d. 11 n. 45)*

28. Taking into account the mission it has been given, every community should after mature deliberation establish a time order for community life. This time order should be approved by the major superior and periodically revised. *(GC32 d. 11 n. 47)*

29. Customs which are more suitable for monastic life shall

not be introduced into our community life, nor those which are proper to seculars; much less, those which manifest a worldly spirit. Let our relationship with all other men be such as can rightly be expected from a man consecrated to God and seeking the good of souls above all things; and it should include a proper regard for genuine fellowship with all other Jesuits. *(GC31 d. 19 n. 7e)*

30. Since our communities are apostolic, they should be oriented toward the service of others, particularly the poor, and to cooperation with those who are seeking God or working for greater justice in the world. For this reason, under the leadership of superiors, communities should periodically examine whether their way of living sufficiently supports their apostolic mission and encourages hospitality. They should also consider whether their style of life testifies to simplicity, justice, and poverty. *(GC32 d. 11 n. 48)*

31. Communities will not be able to witness to Christian love unless each member contributes to community life and gives sufficient time and effort to the task. Only in this way can an atmosphere be created which makes communication possible and in which no one goes unnoticed or is neglected. *(GC32 d. 11 n. 49)*

32. As far as apostolic work or other occupations for the greater glory of God permit it, all of us "esteeming others in their hearts as better than themselves" should be ready to help out in the common household chores. *(GC31 d. 19 n. 7c)*

33. To the extent possible, superiors should strive to build an Ignatian apostolic community in which many forms of open and friendly communication on a spiritual level are possible. Since it is a privileged way to find God's will, the use of communal spiritual discernment is encouraged if the question at issue is of some importance and the necessary preconditions have been verified. *(GC32 d. 11 n. 50)*

34. Solidarity among communities in a province as well as fraternal charity require that communities be open to men of different ages, talent, and work. *(GC32 d. 11 n. 51)*

35. Keeping in mind apostolic poverty and our witness to those among whom we must live, our houses should be made suitable for apostolic work, study, prayer, relaxation of mind and a friendly spirit, so that Jesuits will feel at home in their own house. It can be a great help to the simplicity and intimacy of community life as well as to poverty if the house or place where we live and the house or place where we work or even where we study can be conveniently separated. *(GC31 d. 19 n. 7f)*

Continuing Formation

36. Continuing formation demands that definite periods of time be given to formal courses or simply to private study, whether in theology or other disciplines, as required for one's apostolate. At determined times, all should be given sufficient opportunity for study and for reflection about their apostolic life. *(GC32 d. 6 nn. 20, 35)*